# FRANCE

## Introduction

The tanks employed by France during World War II were greatly minimised by the rigid tactical doctrine that was biased towards infantry support. As the result, the vehicles developed and adopted were generally low-speed and completely unsuited to fast mobile armoured operations. Furthermore, the crews were generally too small in number—thereby requiring of the commanders too many functions under combat situations. Despite these operational misconceptions, the actual engineering and technological design of French tanks was, in general, excellent and represented the very foremost in contemporary research and development. The French armoured forces at the beginning of the war were made up of 2,285 tanks (excluding obsolete models and those deployed in the colonies), comprising 6 basic models: Renault R-35, Hotchkiss H-35, and FCM-36 light tanks (and their derivatives), the Char D, SOMUA S35, and the Char B. There were also a large number of so-called AMRs and AMCs, which were in effect tracked armoured cars. The distribution of these tanks throughout the French Army in June 1940 was as follows: 3 armoured divisions totalling 468 tanks (Chars B1, B1 bis, and H-39); 3 light mechanised divisions totalling 582 tanks (Chars S-35, S-40, H-35, and H-39/40); 5 light cavalry divisions totalling 110 tanks (Chars H-35 and H-39/40); and 25 separate non-divisional tank battalions totalling 1,125 tanks (Chars R-35, H-35, FCM-36, and D2).

# LIGHT TANKS

## *Char Léger Renault FT* (Light Tank Renault FT)

This light tank, which was famous for its exploits during World War I, still remained in service with French armoured units when World War II broke out. It also formed a major part of the tank strengths of several other nations who had adopted it during the early 1930s. The Renault FT light tank was conceived by General Estienne as a light infantry-accompanying tank, and was designed by Renault et Serre in 1916. 3,177 vehicles of this type had been produced by the time of the Armistice in 1918. Between the wars the tank was extensively modified, and during 1931 existing vehicles were re-armed with the 7.5-mm Chatellerault machine-gun in place of the original 8-mm Hotchkiss type. Several variations utilising Kégresse rubber tracks and different forms of armament were developed. 500 Renault FTs were employed during the initial stages of World War II by the French, and then later by the Germans. One of the most prominent of the modifications was the Char Renault BS, mounting a 75-mm gun, a few of which were encountered by the Allies during the invasion of France in June 1944.

**DATA**

CREW  2

WEIGHT  6,700 kg  6.6 tons

HEIGHT  2.14 m  7 ft

LENGTH  4.10 m  13 ft 5½ in

WIDTH  1.74 m  5 ft 8½ in

ENGINE  Renault 4-cyl. water-cooled petrol developing 35 hp

SPEED  Road 10 kmh  6.2 mph

Cross-country 7 kmh  4.4 mph

ROAD RADIUS  60 km  37 miles

ARMAMENT  Either one 37-mm Sa gun or one 7.5-mm Chatellerault MG

ROUNDS CARRIED  240×37 mm

4,800×7.5 mm

ARMOUR THICKNESS  Max 22 mm  0.87 in

Min  6 mm  0.24 in

*Char Léger Renault FT, armed with a 37-mm Sa gun; crew member is using a Fusil Mitrailleur Mle 1924/29 as an anti-aircraft weapon*

*Char Léger Renault FT, armed with a 7.5-mm machine-gun being covered with a camouflage netting on a light tank transporter*

## AMR Renault Modèle 1933 VM (Armoured Reconnaissance Vehicle Renault Model 1933 VM)

As part of the 1931 re-equipment programme, the specifications for a light armoured reconnaissance vehicle (AMR) were laid down on 16 January 1932. Renault produced a vehicle to this specification and after tests with 5 prototypes, over the period 1932 to 1933, the French Army adopted the vehicle as the AMR Renault Modèle 1933 VM. The vehicle was accepted officially on 6 June 1933. A total of 123 were built.

**DATA**
CREW 2
WEIGHT 5,500 kg 5.4 tons
HEIGHT 1.73 m 5 ft 8¼ in
LENGTH 3.5 m 11 ft 5¾ in
WIDTH 1.64 m 5 ft 4½ in
ENGINE Renault 8-cyl. water-cooled petrol
developing 84 hp
SPEED Road 54 kmh 33.6 mph
Cross-country 30 kmh 18.6 mph
ROAD RADIUS 200 km 124.3 miles
ARMAMENT One 7.5-mm machine-gun
ROUNDS CARRIED 2,250
ARMOUR THICKNESS Max 13 mm .51 in
Min 5 mm .20 in

*AMR Renault Modèle 1933 VM*

## AMR Renault Modèle 1935 ZT (Armoured Reconnaissance Vehicle Renault Model 1935 ZT)

The AMR 1933 VM vehicle did not quite come up to requirements, and in 1934 Renault developed a new version. The most fundamental alteration was to locate the engine at the rear (the AMR 1933 VM had been front-engined) to provide better vision for the driver. The running gear was also lengthened to allow a smoother ride across country. Due to the international situation 100 of these vehicles were ordered, and there were 4 versions adopted which differed in their armament. The first had a turret similar to that of the AMR 1933 VM armed with a 7.5-mm machine-gun. The second version had a 13.2-mm Hotchkiss machine-gun in a larger turret. The third version had thicker armour and a 25-mm gun and a 7.5-mm machine-gun in the turret. The fourth version had a fixed superstructure with the same armament as the third version. Altogether 200 AMR 1935s were produced in three separate batches of 100, 30 and 70 respectively.

**DATA**
CREW 2
WEIGHT 6,500 kg 6.4 tons
HEIGHT 1.88 m 6 ft 2¼ in
LENGTH 3.84 m 12 ft 7 in
WIDTH 1.76 m 5 ft 9½ in
ENGINE Renault 4-cyl. water-cooled petrol
developing 82 hp
SPEED Road 60 kmh 37 mph
Cross-country 30 kmh 18.6 mph
ROAD RADIUS 200 km 124.3 miles
ARMAMENT Various (see text)
ROUNDS CARRIED 2,250 (7.5-mm mg version);
1,220 (13.2-mm version);
1,000 (25-mm version)
ARMOUR THICKNESS Max 13 mm .51 in
Min 5 mm .20 in

*AMR 35, armed with 25-mm gun*

*AMR Renault Modèle 1935 ZT, 2nd version, armed with 13.2-mm Hotchkiss machine-gun*

*Fourth version of the AMR 35 with fixed superstructure and armed with a 25-mm gun*

**DATA**

CREW   3

WEIGHT   9,700 kg   9.55 tons

HEIGHT   2.10 m   6 ft 11 in

LENGTH   3.98 m   13 ft

WIDTH   2.07 m   6 ft 9½ in

ENGINE   Renault 8-cyl. water-cooled petrol developing 120 hp

SPEED   Road 40 kmh   25 mph

Cross-country 30 kmh   18.6 mph

ROAD RADIUS   200 km   124.3 miles

ARMAMENT   One 47-mm Sa34 gun and one 7.5-mm mg

ROUNDS CARRIED   Not available

ARMOUR THICKNESS   Max 20 mm   .79 in

Min   5 mm   .20 in

## AMC Renault Modèle 1934 YR (Armoured Combat Vehicle Renault Model 1934 YR)

As a result of the 1931 programme, Renault developed a light armoured combat vehicle for use by the mechanised cavalry. The prototype appeared in October 1933, and the vehicle was officially adopted in 1934. Only 12 of these vehicles were produced due to the decision to adopt the AMC 1935 instead.

*AMC Renault Modèle 1934 YR*

## AMC Renault Modèle 1935 (Armoured Combat Vehicle Renault Model 1935)

**DATA**
CREW 3
WEIGHT 14,500 kg 14.3 tons
HEIGHT 2.51 m 8 ft 3 in
LENGTH 4.78 m 15 ft 8½ in
WIDTH 2.27 m 7 ft 5½ in
ENGINE Renault 4-cyl. water-cooled petrol
    developing 180 hp
SPEED Road 40 kmh 25 mph
    Cross-country 30 kmh 18.6 mph
ROAD RADIUS 200 km 124.3 miles
ARMAMENT Either one 47-mm gun or one 25-mm
    gun, and one 7.5-mm mg
ROUNDS CARRIED Not available
ARMOUR THICKNESS Max 25 mm .98 in
    Min 5 mm .20 in

In 1935 the French cavalry adopted a new, improved model of the AMC, also produced by Renault. It was almost identical to the original model but had a new larger turret (APX 2). Basically the same armament was retained as in the original, the vehicle being referred to as the ACG 1. There was a variant, however, that mounted a 25-mm Hotchkiss gun in place of the 47-mm gun, and this became known as the ACG 2. The AMC 1935 suffered from extreme teething troubles which delayed its entry into service. 100 vehicles were built altogether, later production being taken over by AMX.

*AMC Renault Modèle 1935 (AGGI) with 47-mm gun*

## Auto-mitrailleuse du Corps de Cavalerie

In 1937 twelve ACGI chassis were purchased by the Belgian Ministry of Defence. These vehicles were equipped with Belgian-designed turrets, which had been modified by moving the left-side episcope to the rear and closing up the original opening. They were armed with the FRC 47-mm anti-tank gun and a co-axial 13.2-mm Hotchkiss machine-gun. From September 1939 eight of these vehicles were battleworthy and they were used in action during the 1940 campaign.

*Auto-mitrailleuse du Corps de Cavalerie*

## Char Léger Hotchkiss Modèle 1935 (Light Tank Hotchkiss Model H-35)

**DATA**
CREW 2
WEIGHT 11,300 kg 11.1 tons
HEIGHT 2.13 m 7 ft
LENGTH 4.22 m 13 ft 10 in
WIDTH 1.85 m 6 ft 0¾ in
ENGINE Hotchkiss Model 6L6 6-cylinder
    water-cooled petrol developing 75/120 hp
SPEED Road 28/36 kmh 17.4/22.4 mph
    Cross-country 12/17 kmh 7.5/10.6 mph
ROAD RADIUS 150 km 100 miles
ARMAMENT One 37-mm Sa18 gun and one 7.5-mm
    MG 31
ROUNDS CARRIED 58×37 mm 2,400×7.5 mm
ARMOUR THICKNESS Max 34 mm 1.34 in
    Min 12 mm .47 in

As mentioned under the R-35, the H-35 was a competitor light infantry tank. The first prototype was released on 11 January 1935. The commission testing the two tanks found the H-35 to be better in several respects, but the early production version was grossly underpowered and had a poor cross-country performance. The cavalry accepted the H-35 as their standard light tank in October 1936, and after modification the H-35 Modèle 38 was accepted by the infantry to supplement the R-35. By June 1940 791 H-35s and their derivatives were deployed in French tank units. Later models of the H-35 received the APX-R turret as used on the R-35. Improvements were carried out to the H-35 in February 1939; the 75-hp engine had been considered inadequate and so a more powerful 120-hp engine was utilized. This adaption necessitated modification to the rear hull armour. At first the new tank was designated the H-35 Modèle 38, but later became referred to as the H-35 Modèle 39, and finally just H-39.

*Char Léger Hotchkiss Modèle 1939* ▲

*Char Léger Hotchkiss Modèle 1935* ▶

## DATA

CREW 2
WEIGHT 10,600 kg 10.4 tons
HEIGHT 2.1 m 6 ft 10½ in
LENGTH 4.0 m 13 ft 1½ in
WIDTH 1.85 m 6 ft 0¾ in
ENGINE Renault 4-cyl. water-cooled petrol
developing 82 hp
SPEED Road 19 kmh 11.8 mph
Cross-country 12 kmh 7.5 mph
ROAD RADIUS 140 km 87 miles
ARMAMENT One 37-mm gun (see text) and one
7.5-mm MG31
ROUNDS CARRIED 58×37 mm 2,500×7.5 mm
ARMOUR THICKNESS Max 45 mm 1.77 in
Min 14 mm .55 in

## Char Léger Hotchkiss Modèle H-39/40 (Light Tank Hotchkiss Model H-39/40)

A proportion of H-39s were equipped with new armament, the 37-mm Sa18 gun being replaced by the Sa38 with longer barrel. Trials with this model began in July 1938 and quantity production began in October of the same year. The maximum armour was increased to 40 mm, making the overall weight 12 tons. The ammunition stowage was increased to 100 rounds of 37 mm. In other respects the tank was identical to the H-39.

*Knocked out Hotchkiss Modèle 39/40*
*France 1940*

## Char Léger Renault Modèle R-35 (Light Tank Renault Model R-35)

On 2 August 1933 the French High Command announced a new programme for a light tank, to be armoured against all light anti-tank weapons and capable of supporting the infantry. Several firms submitted proposals, and one of those accepted was that by the Renault firm. This led to the construction of a prototype ZM light tank. Following comparison trials with the Hotchkiss entry (later H-35), which proved unsatisfactory, the Renault design was accepted as the standard light infantry tank on 9 April 1935 and an initial order for 200 was given. The Renault ZM received the designation Char Léger 1935R, though it was usually referred to as the R-35. Early production vehicles were fitted with the L.713 (APX-R) turret mounting the 37-mm Sa18 gun. This was superseded by the L.739 turret with the improved 37-mm Sa18 gun M37. Finally, a small number of R-35s were fitted with the L.767 turret armed with the long-barrelled 37-mm Sa38 gun.

## Char Léger Renault Modèle R-39 (Light Tank Renault Model R-39)

In 1938 several R-35 light tanks were fitted with trench-crossing tails. These have been referred to as R-39s, although no official records have been found to confirm this.

*Renault Modèle R-35*

**DATA**
CREW   2
WEIGHT   10,400 kg   10.24 tons
HEIGHT   2.35 m   7 ft 8½ in
LENGTH   4.58 m   15 ft
WIDTH   2.02 m   6 ft 7½ in
ENGINE   Renault 4-cyl. water-cooled petrol
　　　　　developing 82 hp
SPEED   Road 20 kmh   12.4 mph
　　　　　Cross-country 12 kmh   7.5 mph
ROAD RADIUS   100 km   62 miles
ARMAMENT   One 37-mm Sa38 gun and one 7.5-mm
　　　　　MG31
ROUNDS CARRIED   65×37 mm   3,000×7.5 mm
ARMOUR THICKNESS   Max 58 mm   2.28 in
　　　　　　　　　　　Min 20 mm   .79 in

## *Char Léger Renault Modèle R-40* (Light Tank Renault Model R-40)

This light tank, which was adopted in 1940, was an improved model of the R-35 with a new suspension system. AMX was sub-contracted to provide a new suspension system that would give a better performance cross-country. Two battalions of R-40 saw action in 1940, some armed with the 37-mm Sa38 gun and some fitted with the trench-crossing tail. Later production models of the R-35, equipped with this gun, were also known as R-40.

*Renault Modèle R-40*

## *Char Léger FCM Modèle 1936* (Light Tank FCM Model 1936)

In addition to the Renault and Hotchkiss light tanks, a comparatively small number (100) FCM 36 light tanks were adopted in 1936. This was the first French mass-produced tank to be equipped with a diesel engine. Another novel feature for a French tank at that time was the application of welded armour. It served alongside the R-35 as a light infantry support tank.

DATA

CREW 2
WEIGHT 12,000 kg 11.8 tons
HEIGHT 2.0 m 6 ft 6½ in
LENGTH 4.35 m 14 ft 3¼ in
WIDTH 2.10 m 6 ft 10½ in
ENGINE Berliet 4-cylinder water-cooled diesel
developing 91 hp
SPEED Road 24 kmh 14.9 mph
Cross-country 12 kmh 7.5 mph
ROAD RADIUS 225 km 140 miles
ARMAMENT One 35-mm Sa gun and one 7.5-mm
MG31.
ARMOUR THICKNESS Max 40 mm 1.57 in
Min 13 mm .51 in

*FCM Modèle 1936 being unloaded from tank transporter*

DATA

CREW 3
WEIGHT 14,000 kg 13.8 tons
HEIGHT 2.40 m 7 ft 10½ in (with aerial)
LENGTH 5.76/4.81 m 18 ft 11 in/15 ft 9¼ in (with &
w/o tail)
WIDTH 2.16 m 7 ft 1 in
ENGINE Renault 4-cyl. water-cooled petrol
developing 74 hp
SPEED Road 18 kmh 11.2 mph
Cross-country 10 kmh 6.2 mph
ROAD RADIUS 90 km 56 miles
ARMAMENT One 47-mm Sa34 gun and two
7.5-mm mgs
ROUNDS CARRIED 112×47 mm 5,000×7.5 mm
ARMOUR THICKNESS Max 40 mm 1.57 in
Min 10 mm .39 in

## *Char Léger Renault Modèle D1* (Light Tank Renault Model D1)

During the 1920's Renault had developed a private venture in the form of the NC light tank, which was exported abroad in two basic variants (NC1, NC2). Following the light tank specification laid down in 1926, the NC tank was modified as the NC3. At the end of 1929 the French Army ordered 10 vehicles which were delivered and tested in 1931. Adopted as the Char Léger D1, this tank became the first AFV to be standardised by the French Army after World War I. By 1932 a total of 160 Char D1s had been delivered as light infantry-accompanying tanks. The tank was used operationally by French troops during the fighting in France in 1940 and also later in North Africa.

*Char D1 in action in Tunisia 1942*

7

## Char Léger Renault Modèle D2 (Light Tank Renault Model D2)

### DATA
CREW  3
WEIGHT  19,750 kg  19.4 tons
HEIGHT  2.67 m  8 ft 9 in
LENGTH  5.46 m  17 ft 11 in (w/o tail)
WIDTH  2.22 m  7 ft 3¼ in
ENGINE  Renault 6-cyl. water-cooled petrol
    developing 150 hp
SPEED  Road 23 kmh  14.3 mph
    Cross-country 16 kmh  9.9 mph
ROAD RADIUS  100 km  62 miles
ARMAMENT  One 47-mm Sa34 or Sa35 gun and two
    7.5-mm mgs
ROUNDS CARRIED  120 (47-mm Sa34), 108 (47-mm
    Sa35), 5,000×7.5 mm
ARMOUR THICKNESS  Max 40 mm  1.57 in
    Min 20 mm  .78 in

In 1930 the French infantry requested a vehicle with better armour than the Char D1. This led to the development of the Char D2, which was also built by Renault. The prototype was presented in April 1932 under the designation UZ. After long tests, thwarted with breakdowns, the French Army eventually adopted the tank, 50 being ordered on 19 January 1934. In May 1937 the *Conseil Consultatif de l'Armement* ordered a further 50, which were delivered just before hostilities.

*Char D2. The playing card insignia identified sub-units*

## MEDIUM TANKS

### Char Moyens de Bataille B (Medium Battle Tank B series)

On 12 August 1924 the Director of Infantry requested the provision of 60 tanks (2 battalions of 3 companies each) of a new type of battle tank. On 20 March 1925 General Estienne gathered together a team of tank designers who were given the specifications for the new tank. On 10 February 1926 the characteristics of the new tank were stated explicitly, it now being called *Char de Bataille* (Char B). A contract was placed in March 1927 with the firms of Renault, F.C.M., and F.A.M.H. (St. Chamond) for the production of three prototypes of the Char B. Parent firm was selected as *Atelier de Construction de Rueil* (ARL). The three prototypes tested between 1929 and 1931 had different armour thicknesses and other design changes. Following trials, production of the new tank began at the end of 1934 under the designation Char B1. After the delivery of 35 vehicles, an order was placed for the armour to be increased from 40 mm to 60 mm, resulting in the Char B1-*bis*. To compensate for the extra weight, the engine was up-rated to 307 hp (formerly 250 hp). In 1939 ARL led the design of the final model, the B1-*ter*. This had two diesel engines totalling 350 hp, armour increased to 75 mm, and other improvements. Only 5 vehicles of this latter type were completed. By May 1940 a total of 387 Chars B (all types) were in service with the French Army.

### DATA

| Model B1 | Model B1-*bis* | Model B1-*ter* |
|---|---|---|
| CREW  4 | CREW  4 | CREW  5 |
| WEIGHT  30,000 kg  29.5 tons | WEIGHT  31,500 kg  31 tons | WEIGHT  36,000 kg  35.4 tons |
| HEIGHT  2.16 m  7 ft 1 in | HEIGHT  2.79 m  9 ft 2 in | HEIGHT  2.86 m  9 ft 4½ in |
| LENGTH  6.32 m  20 ft 9 in | LENGTH  6.37 m  20 ft 11 in | LENGTH  6.35 m  20 ft 9¾ in |
| WIDTH  2.50 m  8 ft 2½ in | WIDTH  2.50 m  8 ft 2½ in | WIDTH  2.73 m  8 ft 11½ in |
| ENGINE  Renault 6-cyl. water-cooled petrol developing 250 hp | ENGINE  Renault 6-cyl. water-cooled petrol developing 307 hp | ENGINE  2×Renault 6-cyl. water-cooled diesels developing 175 hp each |
| SPEED  Road 34 kmh  21 mph | SPEED  Road 28 kmh  17.4 mph | SPEED  Road 28 kmh  17.4 mph |
| Cross-country 16 kmh  10 mph | Cross-country 16 kmh  9.9 mph | Cross-country 16 kmh  9.9 mph |
| ROAD RADIUS  180 km  112 miles | ROAD RADIUS  180 km  112 miles | ROAD RADIUS  250 km  156 miles |
| ARMAMENT  One 75-mm Sa35 gun, one 47-mm Sa35 gun, and two 7.5-mm mgs | | |
| ROUNDS CARRIED  75×75 mm | ROUNDS CARRIED  74×75 mm | ROUNDS CARRIED  100×75 mm |
| 55×47 mm | 50×47 mm | 80×47 mm |
| 5,100×7.5 mm | 5,100×7.5 mm | 5,100×7.5 mm |
| ARMOUR THICKNESS  Max 40 mm  1.57 in | ARMOUR THICKNESS  Max 60 mm  2.36 in | ARMOUR THICKNESS  Max 75 mm  2.95 in |
| Min 15 mm  .59 in | Min 22 mm  .87 in | Min 20 mm  .70 in |

*Char Moyens de Bataille B (B1)* ◀

*Char Moyens de Bataille B (B1-bis)* ▶

**DATA**

CREW 3

WEIGHT 19,500 kg 19.2 tons

HEIGHT 2.63 m 8 ft 7½ in

LENGTH 5.38 m 17 ft 8 in

WIDTH 2.12 m 6 ft 11½ in

ENGINE SOMUA 8-cyl. water-cooled petrol developing 190 hp

SPEED Road 47 kmh 29.2 mph

Cross-country 23 kmh 14.3 mph

ROAD RADIUS 250 km 155.4 miles

ARMAMENT One 47-mm Sa35 gun and two 7.5-mm mgs

ROUNDS CARRIED 118 × 47 mm 1,250 × 7.5 mm

ARMOUR THICKNESS Max 40 mm 1.57 in

Min 20 mm .79 in

## *Char de Cavalerie SOMUA 1935S* (Cavalry Tank SOMUA S-35)

This was a medium tank intended for use by the French cavalry units. It resulted from the 1934 programme which specified an armoured combat car armed with a 47-mm or 25-mm gun and a machine-gun, armoured on a 40-mm basis, having a 3-man crew, and a range of 200 kilometres. The SOMUA firm built a cast-steel prototype, which was designated *Auto-mitrailleues de Combat* SOMUA Type AC3 (Armoured Combat Vehicle SOMUA Type AC3). Eventually, the vehicle was redesignated *Char de Cavalerie* S-35. The production vehicle appeared at the beginning of 1935 and received a new turret with a 47-mm Sa35 gun and two 7.5-mm Reibel machine-guns. 261 vehicles were accepted by the French Army. At the beginning of 1940 a modified version was adopted, the SOMUA S-40, with more powerful armament and a new suspension system. The SOMUA tank was considered to be the best tank in the world at the time, and was highly regarded by the Germans.

▲

*Char de Cavalerie SOMUA 1935S. Tunisia 1942*

## Char Lourdes FCM 2C (Heavy Tank FCM 2C series)

General Estienne foresaw the need for a number of ultra-heavy tanks, and 300 were ordered from F.C.M. Work on this tank, designated 2C, was started but the order was reduced to 60 in May 1917. The construction of 10 vehicles was underway when the Armistice was signed, and further orders were dropped. The 10 vehicles were continued with, however, and by 1923 they all had been completed. During 1926 one of these vehicles was re-worked as the Char 2C-*bis* (often erroneously called Char 3C), and was re-armed with a short 155-mm howitzer. The tank had two turrets, the rear one mounting a machine-gun. The Char 2C-*bis* had new engines and heavier armour. Eight of these machines were ready for action in 1940 behind the defensive lines, but were destroyed on their special railway flats by German dive-bombers before they could be deployed in action.

---

**DATA**

| **Char 2C** | **Char 2C-*bis*** |
|---|---|
| CREW 12 | CREW 13 |
| WEIGHT 68,000 kg 66.9 tons | WEIGHT 75,000 kg 73.8 tons |
| HEIGHT 4.15 m 13 ft 7½ in | HEIGHT 4.04 m 13 ft 3 in |
| LENGTH 10.37 m 34 ft | LENGTH 10.27 m 33 ft 8½ in |
| WIDTH 2.97 m 9 ft 8¾ in | WIDTH 2.97 m 9 ft 8¾ in |
| ENGINE 2 × Daimler 6-cyl. water-cooled petrol developing 180 hp (each); later replaced by 2 Maybach 250-hp engines | ENGINE 2 × Sautter-Harlé 6-cyl. water-cooled petrol developing 250 hp (each) |
| SPEED Road 13 kmh 8 mph | SPEED Road 13 kmh 8 mph |
| Cross-country 8 kmh 5 mph | Cross-country 8 kmh 5 mph |
| ROAD RADIUS 150 km 93.2 miles | ROAD RADIUS 150 km 93.2 miles |
| ARMAMENT One 75-mm gun and four 7.5-mm mgs | ARMAMENT One 155-mm howitzer and four 7.5-mm mgs |
| ROUNDS CARRIED 150 × 75 mm 10,000 × 7.5 mm | ROUNDS CARRIED 124 × 55 mm 10,000 × 7.5 m |
| ARMOUR THICKNESS Max 45 mm 1.77 in | ARMOUR THICKNESS Max 50 mm 1.97 in |
| Min 10 mm .39 in | Min 12 mm .47 in |

*FCM 2C knocked out on its railway flat car by German air attacks in 1940*

# POLAND

## Introduction

At the beginning of World War II the Polish Army was not very highly mechanised and possessed only a small tank force comprised mainly of tankettes and light tanks. A series of tankettes was developed on the basis of the British Carden-Loyd Mk VI machine-gun carrier, collectively designated TK, mounting light machine-guns. These were complemented by two models of a light medium tank based on the Vickers 6-ton design and designated 7TP (7-ton Polski). The original 7TP model was twin-turreted and mounted only machine-gun armament, but later a single turreted version appeared equipped with a Bofors anti-tank gun. These vehicles formed the brunt of the Polish armoured forces although several prototype vehicles were under development at the time of the German attack. The lack of tanks and the very bleak international situation compelled the Polish General Staff to seek the purchase of foreign tanks. During 1938 contacts were made with Czechoslovakia which, however, refused to sell Praga and Škoda tanks to Poland. In April 1939 the Polish General Staff finally obtained permission to purchase 100 Renault R-35 tanks from France. The first batch comprising 49 R-35s and 4 H-39s (equivalent to one tank battalion) arrived in Poland by sea in May 1939. Other tanks, in the process of being ferried by land, arrived in Rumania where they remained due to the outbreak of war.

Polish tanks in service at the outbreak of war were as follows: TK.3 (300), TKS (390), and Light Tanks 7TP (170).

## *Mały czołg rozpoznawczy,* TK (Small reconnaissance tank TK)

This was an improved version of the TK.1 and TK.2 vehicles that had originally been developed from the Vickers-Carden-Loyd Mk VI machine-gun carrier. The TK.3 was designed with heavier armour and an enclosed superstructure and put into production; 300 machines were built from 1931-32 onwards. This was the first armoured track-laying machine to be built in quantity in Poland.

DATA
CREW   2
WEIGHT   2,400 kg   2.4 tons
HEIGHT   1.32 m   4 ft 4 in
LENGTH   2.54 m   8 ft 5½ in
WIDTH   1.78 m   5 ft 10 in
ENGINE   Ford Model A developing 40 hp
SPEED   48 kmh   30 mph
ROAD RADIUS   200 km   124.3 miles
ARMAMENT   One 7.92-mm Hotchkiss wz 25 mg
ROUNDS CARRIED   1,800×7.92 mm
ARMOUR THICKNESS   Max 8 mm   .31 in
                                      Min 3 mm   .11 in

*Small reconnaissance tank TK.3*

## *Mały czołg rozpoznawczy, TKS* (Small reconnaissance tank TKS)

Developed in 1933, this was an up-armoured version of TK.3 with thicker armour, a Polish-built Fiat engine, wider tracks and a strengthened suspension. The glacis plate was designed to incorporate a single ball-mounted machine-gun; new vision and sighting devices were also installed. Quantity production of 390 vehicles commenced in February 1934.

DATA
CREW   2
WEIGHT   2,600 kg   2.6 tons
HEIGHT   1.33 m   4 ft 4½ in
LENGTH   2.53 m   8 ft 5 in
WIDTH   1.77 m   5 ft 9½ in
ENGINE   Polski Fiat developing 42 hp
SPEED   40 kmh   25 mph
ROAD RADIUS   180 km   112 miles
ARMAMENT   One 7.92-mm Hotchkiss wz 25 mg
ROUNDS CARRIED   2,000×7.92-mm
ARMOUR THICKNESS   Max 10 mm   .39 in
                                      Min   3 mm   .11 in

*Line-up of TKS tanks*

## TK/TKS z karabinem maszynowym kal. 20 mm FK

From 1936 experiments were made to modify and up-gun the TK and TKS series. These improvements included a redesigned front superstructure and the fitting of a 20-mm FK cannon for an anti-tank role. Twenty of these converted vehicles were in service by August 1939.

*Modified TK.3 with 20-mm FK cannon*

## Czołg lekki 7TP (7-ton Polish light tank)

At the same time as the Carden-Loyd tankettes were purchased in 1929, Poland also obtained from Vickers-Carden-Loyd 36 6-Ton Light Tanks of the type 'E' with the production rights. In 1931 it was decided to design a Polish version using Vickers components and a new engine, the Saurer 6-cylinder diesel of 92 hp. Accepted and put into limited production as the VAU-33 (Vickers-Armstrong-Ursus-33) there were two versions, the VAU-33 *jednowiezowy* (single turret) and the VAU-33 *dwuwiezowy* (twin turret). Some of the original Vickers 'E' type tanks were also converted to VAU-33 standards. During 1934, trials were carried out to improve the VAU-33 before the machine went into full production and subsequently a new design was proposed with a modified rear superstructure to house a Saurer VBLD diesel engine of 110 hp, a stronger suspension, increase in frontal armour and various other modifications.

This new machine was designated *Czołg lekki 7TP* and put into production in 1935. The first of the 7TP series to be built were of the twin-turret type (7TP dw); twenty-two of these were ordered and delivered by March 1936. While the production of the twin-turret model was proceeding, it was decided to introduce a single-turret version carrying a 37-mm Bofors tank gun (7TP jw) but due to production difficulties the first batch of turrets had to be obtained from Bofors; these arrived between February 1936 and January 1937. The first prototype was completed by November 1936 and underwent trials in February 1937. Production commenced in mid-1938 with one major change incorporated: the turret rear was extended to accommodate a radio set.

**DATA 7TP jw**
CREW 3
WEIGHT 9,510 kg 9.36 tons
HEIGHT 2.30 m 7 ft 6½ in
LENGTH 4.88 m 16 ft
WIDTH 2.42 m 7 ft 11½ in
ENGINE Saurer VBLD diesel developing 110 hp
SPEED Road 32 kmh 21 mph
ROAD RADIUS 160 km 99 miles
ARMAMENT 37-mm Bofors wz 37 gun and one
7.92-mm wz 30 Browning mg
ROUNDS CARRIED 80×37 mm
3,960×7.92 mm
ARMOUR THICKNESS Max 17 mm .67 in
Min 5 mm .20 in

*Rear view of Polish twin turret light tanks. The front and rear vehicles are Vickers 6-ton tanks reworked to 7 TP standards; the centre vehicle is a 7 TP dw twin turret type*

*7 TP jw, single turret* ▼

# GREAT BRITAIN

## Introduction

Although Great Britain achieved a lead in tank design during the 1920s and early 30s, this was soon lost to other nations which allocated sufficient budgetary allowances to tank development, such as France and the Soviet Union. Despite a multitude of extremely advanced models, produced up until 1936-37, the mainstays of the British tank force were made up of the light tank Mk VI series and the Vickers medium series—both of which were completely obsolete by that time. With the need to carry out rapid rearmament following the German annexation of Austria and the occupation of Czechoslovakia, the new series of British tanks had many shortcomings. The British tank situation deteriorated still further following Dunkirk, where a very large proportion of all British Army mechanised equipment was abandoned in the wake of the advancing Wehrmacht. Basically, for the duration of World War II the British tank force was made up of three types of tank—Light, Cruiser and Infantry. The light tank did not play a very important role, but the cruiser 'C' (compatible with medium) was evolved for the mobile battle and the infantry 'I' (compatible with heavy) for direct infantry support. Despite the poor start, by the end of the war some fairly good designs had evolved. The cruiser series progressed from the A.13 through the Crusader, Cavalier, Centaur, Cromwell and Comet, the infantry through the A.9, A.10, Valentine, Matilda and Churchill. In general, British tanks of World War II were well-designed and well-armoured and possessed excellent road and cross-country performance. Their weakness, however, lay in their poor firepower and it was not until the introduction of the 17-pounder gun towards the end of the war that British tanks achieved any kind of armament equality with their German counterparts. Of particular interest was the multitude of specialised tanks developed by the British, particularly for the Normandy invasion (D-Day). This tremendous and difficult task required a whole range of specialised tanks for clearing obstacles, crossing gaps, wading, flame-throwing, anti-aircraft defence etc. Most of these were converted from conventional gun-tanks then in use with the British Army, including those obtained through Lend-Lease from the USA and Canada.

## Light Tanks Mks II and VI

The British light tank series emanated from the small Carden-Loyd Mk VII and VIII tanks which were produced by Vickers (who took over Carden-Loyd) in 1929. Through the 1930s the Mk II and III saw service in various forms and a few Mk IIA and IIB vehicles were still equipping the Western Desert Force (later 8th Army) in 1940. The Mk IIAs and IIIs were also used by the South Africans in the Abyssinian campaign of 1941. The Mk II and III had Horstmann suspension with paired road wheels and horizontal coil springs. The Light Tank Mk IV was a more powerful development of the Mk III. The idler wheel was dispensed with and the hull was enlarged. The Light Tank Mk V was similar but had a lengthened hull and a larger turret to accommodate two men. The Mk IV and V entered service in 1935-36 and some remained in service in 1940-41. The most widely used of the Vickers Light Tanks was the last of the series, Mk VI. This also had the larger lengthened hull, and a larger cylindrical turret which accommodated a radio set. The suspension was strengthened and a single return roller was fitted to the hull side. The Mk VIA had a faceted cupola and a double armoured louvre over the radiator. Mk VIB was a simplified production type with changes which included a one-piece radiator louvre and a circular cupola. The light tanks up to Mk VIB were armed with either .303 or Vickers S machine-guns in various combinations, but the final variant, the Light Tank Mk VIC, was more powerfully armed with co-axial 15-mm and 7.92-mm Besa machine-guns. Wider bogies and an improved Meadows engine compensated for the extra weight. On this vehicle the cupola was dispensed with. The Mk VI light tank series were in production during the 1936-40 period and remained in service until 1942.

These light tanks proved largely outmoded by the demands of modern mechanised war. Though intended for Colonial policing and reconnaissance work, the shortage of British cruiser tanks meant that all too often the light tank had to be used in an offensive role for which it was not suited. This was particularly true in France in 1940 where light tanks formed the bulk of British armoured strength. With the increasing availability of cruiser tanks, light tanks were not perpetuated further. They were used operationally in France 1939-40, Greece and Crete; also

**DATA Light Tank Mk VIB**
CREW  3
WEIGHT  5,280 kg  5.2 tons
HEIGHT  2.22 m  7 ft 3½ in
LENGTH  3.95 m  12 ft 11½ in
WIDTH  2.06 m  6 ft 9 in
ENGINE  Meadows developing 88 hp
SPEED  Road  56 kmh  35 mph
       Cross-country  40 kmh  25 mph
ROAD RADIUS  209 km  130 miles
ARMAMENT  One .50-cal (12.7-mm) and one .303
       (7.7-mm) mgs
       (Mk VIC) One 15-mm Besa and one
       7.92-mm Besa mgs
ROUNDS CARRIED  175×15 mm  2,700×7.92 mm
ARMOUR THICKNESS  Max 14 mm  .55 in
       Min  4 mm  .16 in

*Light Tank Mk VIC, showing 15-mm and 7.92-mm Besa machine-guns*

with the South Africans in the Abyssinian campaign and the Australians during the Syrian campaign of 1941.

*Light Tank Mk VIA in the Western Desert*

## Auto-Blindee Mitrailleuse T15

This was one of a series of Vickers tanks that were built for export. The chassis was similar in design to the British light tanks, but this version was equipped with a high conical turret. Known as the M1934, 42 vehicles were delivered to Belgium during 1935 where they were armed with the 13.2-mm Hotchkiss machine-gun. Some of these saw limited action against the German Army during the 1940 campaign.

*Belgium light tank T.15*

## Light Tank Mk VII Tetrarch

Designed as a private venture by Vickers in 1937, this vehicle featured several innovations that included a heavier main armament than the previous light tanks and a new type of suspension incorporating four large road wheels with the drive to the rear pair. Steering was effected by warping the tracks.

It was offered to and accepted by the War Office in 1938 and put into production in 1940, though orders were cut back when light tanks were dropped from British armoured divisions. The first employment of the Light Tank Mk VII in offensive operations was in 'Ironclad', the invasion of Madagascar on the 5 May 1942.

In the spring of 1942 a batch of Tetrarch tanks were sent to the Soviet Union with a consignment of British tanks which also included Matildas and Valentines. The Tetrarch was subsequently adopted as a glider air-landing tank, the Hamilcar glider being designed specifically to carry it. This was the first tank to go into action by air, being used in this role at the Normandy landings by the 6th Airborne Division. A few were later used with the American M22 Locust tanks in the air assault across the Rhine on 24 March 1945.

A limited number of Tetrarch tanks were armed with the 3-inch howitzer in place of the 2-pdr and these vehicles were designated Tetrarch ICS (Infantry Close Support).

*Tetrarch light airborne tank being loaded into Hamilcar glider*

DATA
CREW 3
WEIGHT 7,620 kg  7.5 tons
HEIGHT 2.12 m  6 ft 11½ in
LENGTH 4.11 m  13 ft 6 in
WIDTH 2.31 m  7 ft 7 in
ENGINE Meadows MAT developing 165 hp
SPEED Road 64 kmh  40 mph
  Cross-country 45 kmh  28 mph
ROAD RADIUS 225 km  140 miles

ARMAMENT One 2-pdr (40-mm) gun and one
  7.92-mm Besa mg
  ICS One 3-inch howitzer and one
  7.92-mm Besa mg
ROUNDS CARRIED 50×40 mm
  2,025×7.92 mm
ARMOUR THICKNESS Max 14 mm  0.55 in
  Min 54 mm  0.16 in

## Cruiser Tank Mk I (A.9)

This vehicle was intended as a replacement for the obsolete medium tanks then in service. The design of the A.9 was undertaken by Sir John Carden of Vickers in 1934, the prototype being completed by April 1936. After a period of further development production commenced in 1937.

Though the A.9 had originally been rated as a medium tank, under the new service concept of Infantry and Cruiser tanks, it was now classed as Cruiser Tank Mark I.

The armament consisted of a main turret with a 2-pdr gun and a co-axial Vickers machine-gun and two auxiliary machine-gun turrets on either side of the driver's position. This was the first British tank to be equipped with a hydraulic-powered traverse system for turret rotation.

A number of Cruiser Mk Is were fitted with the 3.7-in howitzer to enable them, in a close-support role, to fire high explosive or smoke; these vehicles were designated Mk ICS.

Cruiser Tank Mk I saw action in France 1939-40 and in the Western Desert 1939-41.

*Cruiser Tank Mk I in the Western Desert*

DATA

| | | |
|---|---|---|
| CREW 6 | | |
| WEIGHT 12,190 kg 12 tons | | |
| HEIGHT 2.65 m 8 ft 8½ in | | |
| LENGTH 5.79 m 19 ft | | |
| WIDTH 2.50 m 8 ft 2½ in | | |
| ENGINE AEC Type A.179 developing 150 hp | | |
| SPEED Road 40 kmh 25 mph | | |

Cross-country 24 kmh 15 mph
ROAD RADIUS 241 km 150 miles
ARMAMENT One 2-pdr (40-mm) gun and three .303
(7.7-mm) Vickers mgs
ROUNDS CARRIED 100×40 mm
3,000×7.7 mm
ARMOUR THICKNESS Max 14 mm .55 in
Min 6 mm .24 in

## Cruiser Tank Mk II and Mk IIA (A.10)

This vehicle was designed and developed by Sir John Carden at the request of the War Office in May 1934 for an Infantry tank using the A.9 machine as a basis.

The A.10 had the same hull, suspension and power-operated turret as the A.9, but the two auxiliary machine-gun turrets were discarded. To achieve the increased thickness of armour required for this vehicle in its infantry support role, extra armour plates were bolted to the original hull, this being the first occasion that composite armour was employed.

The main armament was a 2-pdr gun with a Vickers co-axial machine-gun. Alongside the driver was an aperture for an additional machine-gun, but this was blanked off and the space used for the stowage of ammunition. The Mk IIA mounted a 2-pdr gun and a co-axial 7.92-mm Besa machine-gun, with a second Besa machine-gun in the mounting alongside the driver. The close support version, Mk ICS, was armed with the 3.7-in howitzer and two Besa machine-guns.

The A.10 saw action in France 1939-40 and in the Western Desert 1939-41.

*Cruiser Tank Mk IIA*

DATA
CREW 5
WEIGHT 13,970 kg 13.75 tons
HEIGHT 2.65 m 8 ft 8½ in
LENGTH 5.59 m 18 ft 4 in
WIDTH 2.53 m 8 ft 3½ in
ENGINE AEC Type A.179 developing 150 hp
SPEED Road 26 kmh 16 mph
Cross-country 12.9 kmh 8 mph
ROAD RADIUS 161 km 100 miles

ARMAMENT One 2-pdr (40-mm) gun and one .303
(7.7-mm) Vickers mg
(Mk IIA) One 2-pdr (40-mm) gun and
two 7.92-mm Besa mgs
ROUNDS CARRIED 100×40 mm
4,050×7.7 or 7.92 mm
ARMOUR THICKNESS Max 30 mm 1.18 in
Min 6 mm .24 in

## Cruiser Tank Mk III (A.13)

The A.13 was an important step in British tank development, since this was the design that initiated the run of Cruiser tanks equipped with the Christie type of suspension. The design originated in 1936 after British War Office observers had witnessed the high speed demonstrations of the BT tanks at the Soviet Army manoeuvres.

The *Bistrokhodny Tank* or Fast Tank had been evolved from a number of tanks that had been purchased by the Russians from the American engineer, J. Walter Christie, the important feature of these machines being the high speed suspension. This consisted of large diameter road wheels on swinging arms controlled by coil compression springs, which could run either with or without tracks.

**DATA**

CREW 4
WEIGHT 14,220 kg 14 tons
HEIGHT 2.59 m 8 ft 6 in
LENGTH 6.02 m 19 ft 9 in
WIDTH 2.54 m 8 ft 4 in
ENGINE Nuffield Liberty V-12 developing 340 hp
SPEED Road 48 kmh 30 mph
　　　Cross-country 38 kmh 24 mph
ROAD RADIUS 145 km 90 miles
ARMAMENT One 2-pdr (40-mm) gun and one .303
　　　(7.7-mm) Vickers mg
ROUNDS CARRIED 87×40 mm
　　　3,750×7.7 mm
ARMOUR THICKNESS Max 14 mm .55 in
　　　Min 6 mm .24 in

A Christie tank was purchased by the British at the end of 1936 from which two prototype A.13 machines were developed.

After various trials and modifications, in which the pitch of the track was shortened and shock absorbers were incorporated in the suspension, the A.13 went into production in 1938, deliveries commencing early in 1939. The power-driven turret was rectangular in shape with sloping front and side plates. The 2-pdr gun and co-axial Vickers .303 machine-gun were carried in a mantlet supported by trunnions in the front turret plate, an arrangement common to most other contemporary tanks.

Used operationally in France 1940 and Libya 1940-41.

*Cruiser Tank Mk III*

**DATA**

CREW 4
WEIGHT 15,040 kg 14.8 tons
HEIGHT 2.59 m 8 ft 6 in
LENGTH 6.02 m 19 ft 9 in
WIDTH 2.54 m 8 ft 4 in
ENGINE Nuffield Liberty V-12 developing 340 hp
SPEED Road 48 kmh 30 mph
　　　Cross-country 22.5 kmh 14 mph
ROAD RADIUS 145 km 90 miles
ARMAMENT One 2-pdr (40-mm) gun and one .303
　　　(7.7-mm) Vickers or 7.92-mm Besa
　　　mg
ROUNDS CARRIED 87×40 mm
　　　3,750×7.7 or 7.92 mm
ARMOUR THICKNESS Max 30 mm 1.18 in
　　　Min 6 mm .24 in

## Cruiser Tank Mk IV and IVA (A.13 Mk II)

The Cruiser Mk IV was basically an up-armoured version of the Mk III, and did in fact have the ordnance designation A.13 Mk II. This version appeared following the decision in 1939 to increase the armour basis of Cruiser tanks to 30 mm.

The extra armour plating was mainly on the nose, glacis and turret front; another feature was the addition of V-section armour plating on the turret sides. This resulted in the characteristic undercut sides, the feature by which the Mk IV could be distinguished from the Mk III (A.13 Mk I). The Mk IVA designation was given to late production vehicles which had the Vickers co-axial machine-gun replaced by the 7.92-mm Besa. The Mk IVA was also available in limited numbers as a close support vehicle with the 2-pdr gun replaced by a 3-inch howitzer. Some of the A.13 Mk I machines were later reworked with extra armour plates, up to the Mk IV standards; these were externally similar to the Mk IV and could only be distinguished by the early type of gun mantlet as originally fitted to the Cruiser tank Mk III.

*Cruiser Tank Mk IVA in action in the Western Desert*

## Cruiser Tank Mk VI Crusader Mks I-III (A.15)

*Crusader III advancing in Tripolitania* ▲

The Crusader tank was designed between 1938 and 1940 and was the last of the Cruiser series to be developed without consideration of practical experience of modern warfare.

Marks I and II were equipped with a 2-pdr gun and a co-axial 7.92-mm Besa machine-gun in the main turret, with an additional 7.92-mm Besa machine-gun mounted in the front auxiliary turret on the left of the driver. This auxiliary turret was later removed on many of these vehicles and the additional space used for the stowage of ammunition.

The Crusader was first used in action in the Western Desert in June 1941, and it was soon apparent that the vehicle was under-gunned and too thinly armoured.

Increased thickness of armour and the 6-pdr gun was fitted to the Mk III version and many of the Mks I and IIs were later similarly modified. The Crusader remained the standard equipment of the 7th Armoured Division until the Battle of Alamein in which some hundreds of Crusaders took part, many of which were equipped with the 6-pdr gun. Close-support tanks Mk ICS and Mk IICS were armed with the 3-inch howitzer.

DATA

| | | |
|---|---|---|
| CREW | 5 (Mk. I)  3 (Mk III) | |
| WEIGHT | (Mk I) 19,300 kg  19 tons | |
| | (Mk III) 20,070 kg  19.75 tons | (Mk III)  One 6-pdr (57-mm) gun and |
| HEIGHT | 2.23 m  7 ft 4 in | two 7.92-mm Besa mgs |
| LENGTH | 5.99 m  19 ft 8 in | ROUNDS CARRIED (Mk I)  110×40 mm |
| WIDTH | 2.64 m  8 ft 8 in | 5,000×7.92 mm |
| ENGINE | Nuffield Liberty V-12 developing 340 hp | (Mk III) 65×57 mm |
| SPEED | Road 43 kmh  27 mph | 3,755×7.92 mm |
| | Cross-country 24 kmh  15 mph | ARMOUR THICKNESS (Mk I)  Max 40 mm  1.57 in |
| ROAD RADIUS | 204 km  127 miles | Min  7 mm  .28 in |
| ARMAMENT (Mk I) | One 2-pdr (40-mm) gun and | (Mk III)  Max 51 mm  2.0 in |
| | two 7.92-mm Besa mgs | Min  7 mm  .28 in |

*Crusader I on patrol in the desert*

## Cruiser Tank Mk VIII Cromwell (A.27M)

Experience with the Covenanter and Crusader pilot models in late 1940, plus the accrued lessons of the tank actions in France and Libya, led the Ministry of Supply to ask for a heavier cruiser tank which overcame the inherent faults of the existing designs. Thicker armour (65 mm on hull front, 75 mm on turret front), bigger turret ring, a heavier gun (6-pdr) and a more powerful engine, a weight limit of 24 tons, a speed of not less than 24 mph, and above all much better mechanical reliability, were among the improvements requested. One of the designs offered to this specification was by Leyland Motors who had been involved in building Covenanter and Crusader tanks. The Leyland design utilised a chassis similar to the Crusader but was to be powered with a new engine developed by Rolls-Royce, the Meteor, which was an adaptation of the Merlin aero engine. The Merrit-Brown gearbox was another feature of this new design. The Leyland proposal was accepted and designated A.27, the Birmingham Carriage & Waggon Co being

*Centaur IV of the Royal Marine Armoured Support Group*

made parent company of its production group. However, due to the shortage of Merlin engines needed for aircraft production, an interim version of the A.27 was proposed, retaining the Liberty engine of the Crusader, but otherwise identical to the Meteor-engine design. Designed by English Electric, this version was designated A.27L and became known as the Centaur tank. These went into production by the end of 1942. About 950 Centaur tanks were built, with series from I to IV; of these 80 were armed with the 95-mm howitzer for the role of close support. These were used by the Royal Marines Armoured Support Group on the D-Day landings. The A.27M (now known as Cromwell) production started in January 1943, by which time Leyland had become the design and production parents for the entire A.27 series. The Centaur and Cromwell series were structurally similar, with a hull and turret of simple box shape and composite construction—an inner skin with an outer layer of armour bolted on. Driver and co-driver/hull machine-gunner sat in the forward compartment, and the turret crew consisted of the commander, gunner and loader who was also the radio operator. Numerous detail modifications were incorporated during the Cromwell's production run, which ended in 1945. Most important innovation was the introduction of all-welded construction in place of riveting on later models, thus further simplifying mass-production. The Cromwell was numerically the most important British-built cruiser tank of World War II, together with the American-built M4 Sherman, forming the main equipment of British armoured divisions in 1944-45.

## Cromwell I

Original production model with 6-pdr gun and two Besa machine-guns, similar in external appearance to Centaur I.

## Cromwell II

Cromwell I modified by removal of hull machine-gun and fitting of wider tracks—15½ in in place of 14 in.

## Cromwell III

Centaur I re-engined with Meteor to bring it to A.27M standards, fitted to carry auxiliary fuel tanks at the rear. Originally designated Cromwell X.

## Cromwell IV

Centaur III re-engined with Meteor, armed with 75-mm gun and two Besa machine-guns.

DATA   Cromwell IV
CREW  5
WEIGHT   27,940 kg   27.5 tons
HEIGHT   2.51 m   8 ft 3 in
LENGTH   6.35 m   20 ft 10 in
WIDTH   3.05 m   10 ft
ENGINE   Rolls-Royce Meteor V-12 developing 600 hp
SPEED   Road 51.5 kmh   32 mph
      Cross-country 29 kmh   18 mph
ROAD RADIUS   278 km   173 miles
ARMAMENT   QF 75-mm Mk V or VA gun and two 7.92-mm Besa mgs
ROUNDS CARRIED   64×75 mm
      4,950×7.92 mm
ARMOUR THICKNESS   Max 76 mm (101 mm with applique armour)
      3 in (3.98 in)
      Min 8 mm (10 mm on welded variants)
      .31 in (.39 in)

*Cromwell IV moving through a French town during the Normandy campaign*

## Cromwell V

As Cromwell IV but with all-welded hull.

## Cromwell VI

Armed with the 95-mm howitzer replacing the 75-mm gun for close-support role.

## Cromwell VII

Cromwell IV re-worked with applique armour welded on hull front, 15½ in tracks, stronger suspension, reduced final drive ratio to govern down maximum speed to 32 mph. Armed with 75-mm gun and two Besa machine-guns.

## Cromwell VIII

As Cromwell VII but armed with 95-mm howitzer and two Besa machine-guns.

## Cruiser Tank Challenger (A.30)

Design work commenced in May 1942 to provide a vehicle armed with a heavy high-velocity gun to knock out any known German tank. The A.30 as this vehicle was designated was based on a lengthened Cromwell chassis with lightened armour and one extra suspension unit per side.

The fighting compartment was widened to accommodate the specially designed turret to mount the 17-pounder gun.

The Challenger (first known as the Centurion) entered production in March 1944, but only saw action in NW Europe.

**DATA**
CREW 5
WEIGHT 32,000 kg 31.5 tons
HEIGHT 2.79 m 9 ft 1¾ in
LENGTH 8.15 m 26 ft 8¾ in
WIDTH 2.91 m 9 ft 6½ in
ENGINE Rolls-Royce Meteor V-12 developing 600 hp
SPEED Road 51.5 kmh 32 mph
Cross-country 24 kmh 15 mph
ROAD RADIUS 193 km 120 miles
ARMAMENT One 17-pdr (76-mm) gun and one 0.30-cal (7.62-mm) Browning mg
ROUNDS CARRIED 42×76 mm
ARMOUR THICKNESS Max 101 mm 3.98 in
Min 10 mm .39 in

*The Challenger in action in Holland*

## Cruiser Tank Comet (A.34)

This was a heavier, improved version of the Cromwell series, developed to accommodate the new 77-mm gun. This weapon, designed by Vickers-Armstrong, was a new compact version of the 17-pdr with a shorter barrel, shorter breech and lighter in weight.

Its performance and penetrating power were only slightly inferior to those of the 17-pdr. It was intended that the 77-mm gun would fit in the original A.27 type turret with modifications, but in the event an enlarged welded turret was found necessary.

Design of the A.34 was begun in July 1943 and the pilot model was ready for tests by February 1944; as a result of these trials a stronger suspension with the addition of track return rollers was fitted. By this time the A.34 represented a 60 per cent re-design of the A.27 and was virtually a new tank.

Production deliveries commenced in September 1944 and the first A.34s, now named Comet, were issued to the 11th Armoured Division after the Rhine crossing in March 1945.

**DATA**
CREW 5
WEIGHT 33,020 kg 32.5 tons
HEIGHT 2.68 m 8 ft 9½ in
LENGTH 7.66 m 25 ft 1½ in
WIDTH 3.05 m 10 ft
ENGINE Rolls-Royce Meteor V-12 developing 600 hp
SPEED Road 47 kmh 29 mph
Cross-country 26 kmh 16 mph
ROAD RADIUS 198 km 123 miles
ARMAMENT One 77-mm gun and two 7.92-mm Besa mgs
ROUNDS CARRIED 58×77 mm
5,175×7.92 mm
ARMOUR THICKNESS Max 101 mm 3.98 in
Min 14 mm .55 in

*Cruiser Tank Comet*

## Infantry Tank Mk I Matilda I (A.11)

This class of tank stemmed from a General Staff requirement for a tank to support the infantry in the attack.

Specifications requested a heavily armoured vehicle that would be immune to 37-mm anti-tank guns, travel at infantry pace and be armed with a machine-gun to engage enemy troops.

The first pilot model designed by Sir John Carden and built by Vickers-Armstrong was delivered for trials in September 1936 under the code name Matilda for security purposes.

The vehicle had a very small plain hull with exposed tracks and a small cast turret armed with a .303-cal machine-gun.

The suspension consisted of six rubber-tyred and two double steel-tyred road wheels (per side) in two bogie frames supported by semi-elliptic laminated springs. By the outbreak of war some 90 had been built. The 4th Bn RTC were equipped with the Mk I tanks in France from September 1939 until Dunkirk, but none of these machines were saved. Due to the lack of an anti-tank weapon for use against hostile tanks, some Mark Is were fitted with the .50 Vickers machine-gun during their period in France. Production of the Infantry Tank Mk I ceased in August 1940 after 139 had been built.

*Infantry Tank Mk I Matilda I in France 1939-40*

**DATA**

CREW  2

WEIGHT  11,180 kg  11 tons

HEIGHT  1.87 m  6 ft 1½ in

LENGTH  4.85 m  15 ft 11 in

WIDTH  2.29 m  7 ft 6 in

ENGINE  Ford V-8 developing 70 hp

SPEED  Road 12.9 kmh  8 mph

    Cross-country 9 kmh  5.6 mph

ROAD RADIUS  129 km  80 miles

ARMAMENT  One .303-cal (7.7-mm) mg

ROUNDS CARRIED  4,000×7.7 mm

ARMOUR THICKNESS  Max 60 mm  2.36 in

    Min 10 mm  .39 in

## Infantry Tank Mk II Matilda II (A.12)

The need to provide an improved version of the small Infantry Tank Mk I, with room for an extra crew member, a 2-pdr gun and a better speed (of up to 15 mph) led to the development of a considerably larger vehicle. This came about since it was impossible to fit a turret able to mount a 2-pdr gun on the extremely small dimensions of Infantry Tank Mk I. Thus the Mechanisation Board drew up a completely new design, Infantry Tank Mk II, with extremely heavy armour on a 60 mm basis. Box bogie suspension was used to support the heavy weight of the new design, and armoured side skirts with prominent mud chutes were a distinctive feature. A readily available AEC commercial type of diesel engine was utilised due to the urgency of the design, though in a later version (Mk IIA*) a Leyland diesel was used. The actual layout closely followed that of the Medium Tank A.7 which had been built as a prototype in 1929-32 but not produced. The first pilot model was ready for trials by April 1938 and production began in the following year. Armed with a 2-pdr gun and a co-axial .303 Vickers machine-gun in a cast three-man turret, the Mk II Infantry Tank was the most powerful tank in service at that period. The Mk II was sometimes known as the Matilda senior, but when the Mk I was withdrawn from service after Dunkirk the name Matilda was officially adopted.

The Matilda II was first used in action at Arras, France, in May 1940 and proved very successful in combat. During the fighting in the Western Desert in 1940, it was the best-armed and -armoured of the tanks engaged and only the German 8.8-cm Flak gun in mid-1941 was able to penetrate the A.12's armour at long range. As the turret ring was too small to allow a 6-pdr gun to be fitted, this led to the eventual withdrawal of Matildas from tank brigades; Alamein was the last major battle in which it was used. The Matilda also saw service in the Eritrean campaign, Crete and in the South West Pacific area with the Australian army. It was supplied to the Soviet Union. A number of Matildas captured by the Germans in the fighting in the Western Desert were taken into service and used by them.

## Matilda II, Infantry Tank Mk IIA

Similar to Matilda II, but with Besa 7.92-mm machine-gun instead of Vickers.

**DATA**

CREW  4

WEIGHT  26,950 kg  26.5 tons

HEIGHT  2.51 m  8 ft 3 in

LENGTH  5.61 m  18 ft 5 in

WIDTH  2.59 m  8 ft 6 in

ENGINE  Matilda I, II  2×AEC, 87 hp each

    Matilda III, IV  2×Leyland, 95 hp each

SPEED  Road 24 kmh  15 mph

    Cross-country 12.9 kmh  8 mph

ROAD RADIUS  257 km  160 miles

ARMAMENT  One 2-pdr (40-mm) gun and one 7.92-mm Besa mg

ROUNDS CARRIED  92×40 mm

    2,925×7.92 mm

ARMOUR THICKNESS  Max 78 mm  3.07 in

    Min 13 mm  .51 in

*Infantry Tank, Mk II Matilda II, operating in the Tobruk area*

## Matilda III, Infantry Tank Mk IIA*

As Matilda IIA but with two Leyland diesels of 95 hp each.

## Matilda III CS

Matilda III with 3-in howitzer instead of 2-pdr gun.

## Matilda IV, Infantry Tank Mk IIA**

As Matilda III, but with improved Leyland engines, and auxiliary fuel tanks at the rear.

## Matilda IV CS

Matilda IV armed with a 3-in howitzer.

## Matilda V

As Matilda IV, but with improvements to gearbox and gear shift.

## Infantry Tank Mk III Valentine

When Infantry Tank Mk II production commenced, Vickers were asked to join the manufacturing group. Instead they chose to offer the War Office their own design of Infantry Tank that was based on experience gained from the development and manufacture of the A.9 and A.10 Cruiser Tanks. Vickers submitted their proposal two days before St Valentine's Day, 1938, hence the name. The proposal was for a 3-man Infantry Tank, weighing 14-15 tons with an armour basis of 60 mm, designed for rapid production, both from the machinery and assembly point of view, and was to be based on components which had been used with complete satisfaction in the A.9 and A.10 vehicles. There was a delay in official ordering, however, and only when war became inevitable was an order placed in July 1939. The first production vehicles appeared in May 1940; in this case no pilot model was built. This new infantry tank was based on the chassis, suspension and drive train of the A.10, but had a new superstructure and turret; this was the two-man type that necessitated the commander acting as loader for the 2-pdr gun. Observation for both commander and gunner was provided by Vickers type periscopes giving all-round vision. The turret could be rotated either

DATA   Valentine I
CREW   3
WEIGHT   16,260 kg   16 tons
HEIGHT   2.28 m   7 ft 5½ in
LENGTH   5.41 m   17 ft 9 in
WIDTH   2.63 m   8 ft 7½ in
ENGINE   AEC developing 135 hp
SPEED   Road 24 kmh   15 mph
         Cross-country 12.9 kmh   8 mph
ROAD RADIUS   145 km   90 miles
ARMAMENT   One 2-pdr (40-mm) gun and one
         7.92-mm Besa mg
ROUNDS CARRIED   79×40 mm
         3,150×7.92 mm
ARMOUR THICKNESS   Max 65 mm   2.56 in
         Min   8 mm   .31 in

*Valentine Is of the 6th Armoured Division on manoeuvres in England 1941*

manually or by electrical power traverse controlled by the gunner. The driver was situated in the central position at the front of the machine, being given maximum vision in the closed-down position by two Vickers periscopes fitted in addition to the bullet-proof glass-protected slit type forward look-out. The engine and transmission compartment were at the rear end, isolated from the fighting compartment by a fire-proof bulkhead. The fuel tanks were enclosed in a leakproof sub-compartment of the main engine room. In late 1940, Valentines entered full service and some were used in the cruiser tank role to help overcome shortages. The Valentine first saw service in the Western Desert and was used with distinction throughout the campaign, proving to be a good reliable gun platform. Also used operationally in North Africa, Madagascar 1942, Pacific area with New Zealand troops. Canadian-built Valentines VI and VII were supplied to the Soviet Union.

By late 1942 the Valentine was largely obsolete due to its low speed and small turret which restricted the fitting of a larger calibre gun. Valentines III and V had the turret modified to accommodate three men (a loader, in addition to commander and gunner), but the third turret member was dropped when the 6-pdr gun was fitted in later marks. The 6-pdr gun was introduced into production Valentines from March 1942. Other modifications included improved engine installation (GMC diesel units) and a change over from all-riveted to all-welded construction. The final production version in the Valentine series was the Valentine XI; this vehicle was armed with the British 75-mm gun in a specially adapted turret.

### Infantry Tank Mk III* Valentine II

As Valentine I, but with AEC diesel engine (131 hp) replacing petrol engine. Vehicles for desert service equipped with sand shields and jettisonable long-range fuel tanks.

### Valentine III

As Valentine II, but with turret modified to take a third crew member. New turret front with improved mantlet; commander's hatch set towards rear of turret.

*Valentine III. Turret modified to take one extra crew member*

### Valentine IV

As Valentine II, but with GMC diesel engine (138 hp) replacing AEC unit.

### Valentine V

Similar to Valentine III but motive power supplied by GMC diesel engine.

### Valentine VI

Canadian-built model, externally similar to Valentine IV with GMC diesel. In production late 1941. Nose plate cast instead of bolted as on British vehicles. Browning .30-cal machine-gun replaced 7.92-mm Besa.

*Valentine IX*

### Valentine VII

Improved Valentine VI built in Canada with different radio and detailed internal changes.

### Valentine VIIA

Improved Canadian-built Valentine VII, with jettisonable fuel tanks, studded tracks and protective cages over headlamps. The whole production of Canadian-built Valentines, except for the first 30 that were held back for training, was supplied to the Soviet Union.

### Valentine VIII

Valentine III up-gunned with a 6-pdr replacing the 2-pdr and co-axial machine-gun in a redesigned two-man turret.

### Valentine IX

Valentine V up-gunned with a 6-pdr replacing the 2-pdr and co-axial machine-gun in a resdesigned two-man turret.

### Valentine X

As Valentines VIII and IX but with co-axial 7.92-mm Besa machine-gun and up-rated GMC diesel engine (165 hp). In production 1943.

### Valentine XI

Similar to Valentine X, but with British 75-mm gun replacing 6-pdr, and cast nose.

*Valentine XIs operating as a battery commander's vehicles with SP (17-pdr) Anti-Tank regiment*

## Infantry Tank Mk IV Churchill (A.22)

This vehicle was developed jointly by the War Mechanisation Board and Vauxhall Motors Ltd. In general shape, overall dimensions and transmission details it was based on its predecessor, 'A.20', a vehicle that had been projected in 1939 as a heavily armoured Infantry Tank.

The first 14 production models were delivered in June 1941 from an order that had been placed while the vehicle was still on the drawing board. The power plant was designed to be as compact as possible; the radiators and petrol tanks were placed alongside the engine and protected by heavy armour plating against splash. The transmission featured the Merritt-Brown four-speed gearbox which provided controlled differential steering; the Churchill being the first production vehicle to use this. Panniers were provided at each side of the hull, between the upper and lower runs of track; these were used for the stowage of equipment.

The tank was carried on 22 bogies (11 each side), each independently sprung, with steel articulated link tracks that were spudded or webbed. Double doors were installed in the roof above the drive and front gunner as escape hatches, and a square door in each of the hull sides provided access to the driver's compartment. Periscopes were mounted in the hull roof for the driver and front gunner and in front of the turret.

Armament for the Churchill I consisted of a 2-pdr (40-mm) QFSA gun and a 7.92-mm Besa machine-gun co-axially mounted in the turret and a 3-inch QFSA howitzer in the front hull plate. A 2-inch smoke mortar was mounted on the turret roof. Due to the rushed development programme of this vehicle there were numerous defects in the design leading to frequent breakdowns with the early marks.

*Churchill I of Canadian Armoured Regt on large-scale offensive exercises in England 1941*

## Churchill II

This model had the 3-inch howitzer removed from the hull front and replaced by a 7.92-mm Besa machine-gun. A variation of the Churchill II was the close-support version, Churchill IICS, which simply changed over the gun disposition of the Churchill I, so that the 3-inch howitzer was carried in the turret and the 2-pdr gun in the hull.

*Churchill II. Compare 2-pdr gun with size of tank*

CREW   5
WEIGHT   39,620 kg   39 tons
HEIGHT   2.97 m   9 ft 9 in
LENGTH   7.47 m   24 ft 6 in
WIDTH   2.74 m   9 ft
ENGINE   Bedford Twin-Six developing 350 hp
SPEED   Road 24.9 kmh   15.5 mph
        Cross-country 12.9 kmh   8 mph
ROAD RADIUS   145 km   90 miles
ARMAMENT   One 6-pdr (57-mm) M5 gun and two
          7.92-mm Besa mgs
ROUNDS CARRIED   84×57 mm
                 6,975×7.92 mm
ARMOUR THICKNESS   Max 101 mm   3.98 in
                   Min   16 mm   .63 in

# Churchill III

This version appeared in 1942, armed with a 6-pdr in a new type of welded turret. In addition this vehicle was fitted with full track covers, new air intake louvres and other improvements. Used in action during the raid on Dieppe on 19 August 1942 when a small number of Churchill Is were also involved. In action during the Tunisian Campaign 1942-43 and supplied to the Soviet Union in 1942.

*Churchill III with welded turret and armed with 6-pdr gun in action in Tunisia*

# Churchill IV

Appeared concurrent with the Churchill III. Though armed with the 6-pdr gun, the Churchill IV was fitted with a cast turret which offered armour protection slightly superior to that of the welded type. The gun was either the 6-pdr QF Mk 3 or Mk 5, the latter being distinguished by its noticeably longer barrel and counter-weight. Used operationally in Tunisia 1942-43.

*Churchill IV, cast turret and 6-pdr gun moving through the ruins of a French town*

# Churchill IV (Na.75)

During January 1943, the workshops of the armoured brigades of the 1st Army in Tunisia converted 120 Churchill IVs to carry the 75-mm M3 gun taken from wrecked Sherman tanks. This was to enable the tank to fire high-explosive shells; the British 2-pdr and 6-pdr guns fired only AP (armour-piercing shot). These were the first British tanks to take guns of this calibre into action where they were used with great success in the Sicily and Italian campaigns. The N.A.75 (North Africa) remained in service until 1945.

*Churchill IV (NA 75) firing on German lines in Italy*

## Churchill V

This was the same basic vehicle as the Churchill IV, but fitted with a QF 95-mm tank howitzer Mk I for the close-support role. In operations in North Africa, Italy and North West Europe.

*Churchill V (95-mm howitzer)*

## Churchill VI

This was similar to the Churchill IV, but with a British 75-mm gun replacing the 6-pdr gun. In production during 1943.

## Churchill VII (A.22F/A.42)

This was a redesigned version of the Churchill with thicker armour, a heavier suspension and improved gear box. The square side escape hatches were replaced by circular types that were intended to reduce the armour weakness in these areas, and the drivers vision hatch in the vertical front plate was also replaced by a circular hatch. The turret was a complete redesign, having cast sides and a welded roof. Improved vision was provided for the commander by the installation of a raised vision-block circular cupola in place of the previous rotating square hatch. This model entered production at the end of 1943 and was the principal British heavy tank to take part in the invasion of Europe in June 1944, and in subsequent 1944-45 campaigns. Designated A.22F, this vehicle was redesignated A.42 in 1945.

*Churchill VII*

DATA **Churchill VII and VIII**
CREW  5
WEIGHT  41,660 kg  41 tons
HEIGHT  3.45 m  11 ft 4 in
LENGTH  7.44 m  24 ft 5 in
WIDTH  2.74 m  9 ft
ENGINE  Bedford Twin-Six developing 350 hp
SPEED  Road 20 kmh  12.5 mph
      Cross-country 12.9 kmh  8 mph
ROAD RADIUS  145 km  90 miles
ARMAMENT  Churchill VII  One 75-mm gun and
          two 7.92-mm Besa mgs
          Churchill VIII  One 95-mm howitzer
          and two 7.92-mm Besa mgs
ROUNDS CARRIED  Churchill VII  84×75 mm
              6,525×7.92 mm
              Churchill VIII  60×95 mm
              6,525×7.92 mm
ARMOUR THICKNESS  Max 152 mm  5.98 in
                  Min  25 mm  .98 in

## Churchill VIII

This was the final main production version of the Churchill as a combat tank, and was identical in all respects to the Churchill VII except for the main armament, a 95-mm howitzer replacing the 75-mm gun.

## Re-worked Churchill models

With the introduction of the Churchill VII in November 1943, work was started to convert models III, IV, V and VI to Churchill VII standards. Most of this conversion work was carried out in REME workshops. Retrospective fittings included later models of the 6-pdr or 75-mm guns, Churchill VII type vision cupolas and sights, and applique armour. These re-worked and updated Churchills appeared from early 1945 onwards.

## Churchill IX

Churchill III and IV with heavier composite cast/welded VIII type turret, reinforced roof and re-armoured with applique armour consisting of thicker front plates and the addition of skirting plates to the hull. Ordnance QF 6-pdr Mk 3 or Mk 5 was fitted.

## Churchill IX LT

As for Churchill IX but retaining the original light turret.

## Churchill X

This was the Churchill VI re-worked with heavier composite turret, reinforced roof and re-armoured with applique side armour. Also fitted with new visor and glacis plate, heavy suspension units and H41 gearbox as in the Churchill VII. Armed with the QF 75-mm Mk 5 or Mk 5A gun.

## Churchill X LT

As for Churchill X but retaining the original light turret.

## Churchill XI

Re-worked Churchill V tanks incorporating a heavier composite turret, applique side armour, thicker front plates, a reinforced roof and the addition of skirting plates to the hull. The QF 95-mm Howitzer Mk I remained the main armament on this version.

# SOVIET UNION
## Introduction

The majority of the Soviet tanks employed during the early operations of the German campaign in the Soviet Union (summer 1941) were types produced under the Second Five-year Plan and were already outdated by the beginning of World

War II. There were an estimated 21-24,000 tanks available to the Soviet Union in June 1941, of which the Germans destroyed over 17,500 within the first three months of operations.

Despite the fact that most of the Soviet armour was old, the Russians were in the process of introducing new models (T-34, KV, T-40 and T-60) at the time of the German attack, and these were excellent tanks all around. The T-34 and KV tanks remained virtually unchanged throughout the entire war and it took only minor modification to maintain their qualitative superiority over the German machines. When the war terminated the Soviet Union had virtually discarded the light tank altogether, but had retained their T-34 medium (now up-gunned to 85-mm) and redesigned their KV heavy model into the 'Iosef Stalin' mounting a 122-mm gun.

With the tremendous losses in tanks during the first period of the war and the necessity to evacuate almost their entire western tank industries to the east, the Soviets were unable to reach numerical parity with the Germans before 1943. For this reason the Russians were forced to utilise their armour during this defensive period purely as infantry support. As soon as production picked up, however, they began to form larger units—firstly, tank corps, and later tank armies. The quality of these large Soviet tank formations had improved considerably by the end of the war, but their performance was restricted greatly by the lack of military transport.

## *Lyokhy Tank T-26* (Light Tank T-26 series)

As was the case with many other Soviet tanks of the 1930s, the T-26 light tank was developed from a British model, in this case the famous 6-ton light tank built by Vickers-Armstrong Ltd. This model was developed as the basic light infantry-support tank to replace the obsolete MS model, and remained in mass-production throughout the period 1931-40. Altogether more than 12,000 of these vehicles, in multiplicity of models, were manufactured. During 1930 a group of engineers in the Experimental Design Department (OKMO) at the *Bolshevik* Factory in Leningrad, directed by N.V. Barikov and S.A. Ginzburg, manufactured 20 similar vehicles under the designations TMM-1 and TMM-2. Following comparison trials with Soviet-designed models (T-19 and T-20), on 13 February 1931, the Vickers design was accepted by the Revolutionary Military Council (Revvoensovet) for adoption by the Red Army. After minor alterations by the engineer Zigelya, the vehicle was standardised as the T-26. During the following year mass-production began at several factories. Tanks of the first series had two juxta-opposed turrets that could mount a multiplicity of armament combinations. For commanders there was a special version with radio called T-26TU. A companion version, with one turret removed and the other mounting a new long-barrelled 37-mm gun was scheduled for adoption by the Red Army, but only a few were produced due to the decision to adopt a single-turreted model with a larger turret. Mass-production of the single-turreted model began in 1933. Original models were armed with the new 37-mm gun but eventually this was replaced by the 45-mm gun. In 1938, as a result of the fighting against the Japanese in the Far East, a new welded version of the single-turreted model was developed designated T-26S. Some of the earlier models were also retrofitted with the turret of this tank. During service with the Red Army the T-26 underwent many alterations and modifications and several special-purpose vehicles were developed around it.

DATA

CREW 3

WEIGHT 8,000-9,500 kg 7.9-9.35 tons
(depending on model)

HEIGHT 2.08-2.33 m 6 ft 8¾ in-7 ft 7¾ in
(depending on model)

LENGTH 4.62-4.88 m 15 ft 2 in-16 ft 0 in
(depending on model)

WIDTH 2.41-2.44 m 7 ft 11 in-8 ft 0 in
(depending on model)

ENGINE T-26 4-cyl. air-cooled petrol developing 91 hp

SPEED Road 28-32 kmh 17.4-20 mph
(depending on model)
Cross-country 20 kmh 12.4 mph

ROAD RADIUS 100-225 km 62-140 miles
(depending on model)

ARMAMENT Various-see above

ROUNDS CARRIED Various, according to armament

ARMOUR THICKNESS Max 25 mm .98 in
Min 6 mm .24 in

*Light Tank T-26 followed by the twin turret version*

*Commanders' version of the T-26 (T-26TU)*
▼

*Light Tank T-26S*

**DATA**
CREW  2
WEIGHT  3,200 kg  3.15 tons
HEIGHT  1.82 m  5 ft 11¾ in
LENGTH  3.75 m  12 ft 3¼ in
WIDTH  2.00 m  6 ft 7 in
ENGINE  GAZ-AA 4-cyl. water-cooled petrol
    developing 40 hp
SPEED  Road 35 kmh  21.8 mph
    Cross-country 25 kmh  15.5 mph
    Water 4 kmh  2.5 mph
ROAD RADIUS  185 km  115 miles
WATER OPERATION  12 hours
ARMAMENT  One 7.62-mm DT mg
ROUNDS CARRIED  500 rounds.
ARMOUR THICKNESS  Max 9 mm  .35 in
    Min 4 mm  .16 in

## *Lyokhy Plavayushchy Tank T-37* (Light Amphibious Tank T-37 series)

During 1930 some examples of the Carden-Loyd light amphibious tank (A-4E11) were purchased in England. A group of engineers at Factory No. 37 in Memory of S. Ordzhonikidze in Moscow, directed by N.A. Astrov, developed a series of experimental vehicles of this type. After unsuccessful tests with a number of experimental models, on 11 August 1933 the Red Army officially adopted the T-37 light amphibious tank for use by reconnaissance sub-units. Productions began at Factory No. 37. In the meantime, another group of engineers under N.N. Koziryev carried out improvements to the design, resulting in the variant designated T-37A. Since the original vehicle never entered service, however, the suffix A was dropped and the variant became referred to purely as the T-37. Mass-production of the tank began towards the end of 1933 and continued until the end of 1936 when the improved T-38 type appeared. Altogether about 1,200 vehicles of the T-37 type were built in various models. Platoon and company commanders' tanks, designated T-37U or T-37TU, were provided with radio equipment and the characteristic hand-rail aerial around the hull.

*Light Amphibious Tank T-37TU*

## *Lyokhy Plavayushchy Tank T-38* (Light Amphibious Tank T-38)

This light tank, which was a successor to the earlier T-37 light amphibious tank, was accepted for adoption by the Red Army during 1936. It was designed by a group of engineers at the Factory No. 37 in Moscow, under the direction of N.

**DATA**

CREW  2

WEIGHT  3,280 kg  3.23 tons

HEIGHT  1.74 m  5 ft 8½ in

LENGTH  4.05 m  13 ft 3½ in

WIDTH  2.51 m  8 ft 3 in

ENGINE  GAZ-AA 4-cyl. water-cooled petrol developing 40 hp (T-38-M2 had GAZ-M1 4-cyl. water-cooled petrol developing 50 hp)

SPEED  Road 45 kmh  28 mph

Cross-country 25 kmh  15.5 mph

Water 6 kmh  3.7 mph

ROAD RADIUS  250 km  155.7 miles

WATER OPERATION  12 hours

ARMAMENT  One 7.62-mm DT mg

ROUNDS CARRIED  1,512×7.62-mm

ARMOUR THICKNESS  Max 9.5 mm  .37 in

Min  4.0 mm  .16 in

Astrov. In essence the tank was a thoroughly modernised T-37, being lower, faster and having an improved hull and re-located turret (to the opposite side of the vehicle). From 1936 onwards the T-38 replaced the T-37 in production. During 1938 a modified variant with a more powerful 50 hp engine and new transmission was adopted as the T-38-M2. Like the T-37, from 1937 the T-38 formed the basic armoured equipment of the reconnaissance sub-units in armoured, infantry and cavalry units. It was also adopted by the Air-Landing Corps. Production of the vehicle terminated in 1939, although the vehicle continued in service until total replacement by the T-40 light amphibious tank.

*Light Amphibious Tank T-38*

## *Lyokhy Plavayushchy Tank T-40* (Light Amphibious Tank T-40)

**DATA**

CREW  2

WEIGHT  5,590 kg  5.5 tons

HEIGHT  2.12 m  6 ft 11½ in

LENGTH  4.43 m  14 ft 6¼ in

WIDTH  2.51 m  8 ft 3 in

ENGINE  GAZ-202 6-cyl. water-cooled petrol developing 85 hp

SPEED  Road 45 kmh  28 mph

Cross-country 30 kmh  18.6 mph

Water 10 kmh  6.2 mph

ROAD RADIUS  350 km  217.5 miles

ARMAMENT  Either one 12.7-mm DShK or 20-mm ShVAK-20 and one 7.62-mm DT mg

ROUNDS CARRIED  550×12.7/20 mm

2,016×7.62 mm

ARMOUR THICKNESS  Max 13 mm  .51 in

Min  6 mm  .24 in

As the result of the 1939-40 tank programme, the Red Army received a new amphibious light tank to replace the obsolete T-38 model. This was designated the T-40, and first issued to reconnaissance and armoured liaison units at the beginning of 1941. The tank was a complete departure from previous Soviet practice, in that it employed fully independent torsion-bar suspension and welded armour. In order to maintain the amphibious capability the tank was fairly thinly armoured. The original T-40 models were armed with a 12.7-mm heavy machine-gun and a co-axial 7.62-mm DT machine-gun, but about the time of the introduction of the T-60 light tank some T-40s were re-armed with the 20-mm ShVAK-20 cannon. An improved model, sometimes referred to as the T-40A, was introduced during 1941 and had certain minor modifications. During 1942 the T-40S which had greatly increased armour was placed in limited production. Due to the increased weight, however, the tank was no longer amphibious and consequently the water-propulsion and steering components were omitted.

*Light Amphibious Tank T-40*

## Lyokhy Tank T-50 (Light Tank T-50)

The T-50 light tank was designed as a replacement for the T-26 and BT tanks, being intended to support infantry and to carry out reconnaissance missions. Like the T-34 it was characterised by its greatly inclined armour, which was of equal thickness throughout. Due to its similarity in appearance and overall design to the KV heavy tank the T-50 was often referred to as the *'Mali Klim'* (Little Klim). A special diesel engine was developed for this vehicle, but since the tank was complex and required as much production effort as the T-34 medium it was discontinued after only 65 vehicles had been delivered to the Red Army.

**DATA**
CREW 4
WEIGHT 13,500 kg 13.3 tons
HEIGHT ·2.33 m 7 ft 7½ in
LENGTH 5.57 m 18 ft 3¼ in
WIDTH 2.66 m 8 ft 8¾ in
ENGINE GAZ V-4 4-cyl. water-cooled diesel
developing 300 hp
SPEED Road 53 kmh 33 mph
Cross-country 40 kmh 25 mph
ROAD RADIUS 350 km 217.5 miles
ARMAMENT One 45-mm gun and one 7.62-mm DT mg.
ROUNDS CARRIED 150×45 mm 4,000×7.62 mm
ARMOUR THICKNESS Max 37 mm 1.46 in
Min 12 mm .47 in

*Light Tank T-50*

## Lyokhy Tank T-60 (Light Tank T-60)

In 1941 the Red Army adopted the T-60 light tank as a replacement for the T-40 light amphibious tank. In this case, however, the need for heavier armour resulted in the tank being non-amphibious. Difficulty was experienced in the provision of more powerful armament. Soviet engineers attempted to mount a 37-mm gun but, even with reduced charge rounds, the turret ring was unable to absorb the recoil of this weapon. Due to the military situation there was no time to evolve a lighter tank gun and the Soviet armament designers Shpitalny and Vladimirov were given the task of adapting their high-velocity 20-mm ShVAK aircraft cannon for the T-60. This was accomplished in a very short time, and tests showed that armour-piercing incendiary rounds fired by the 20-mm ShVAK cannon could penetrate the same armour as the original 37-mm gun. The new T-60 was accepted in armament and ordered in production in November 1941; over 6,000 were completed and delivered before replacement by the T-70. The vehicle was issued to reconnaissance units and also to infantry formations for direct support in combat. An improved model of the T-60 was produced in late 1941, often referred to as T-60A. This vehicle had increased armour, but the main difference was the substitution of solid road wheels for the earlier spoked type.

**DATA**
CREW 2
WEIGHT 5,750 kg 5.66 tons
HEIGHT 1.89 m 6 ft 2½ in
LENGTH 4.30 m 14 ft 1 in
WIDTH 2.46 m 8 ft 0¾ in
ENGINE GAZ-202 6-cyl. water-cooled petrol
developing 70 hp
SPEED Road 44 kmh 27.3 mph
Cross-country 30 kmh 18.6 mph
ROAD RADIUS 614 km 382 miles
ARMAMENT One 20-mm ShVAK cannon and one
7.62-mm DT mg
ROUNDS CARRIED 780×20 mm 945×7.62 mm
ARMOUR THICKNESS Max 20 mm .79 in
Min 7 mm .28 in

*Light Tank T-60*

*Light Tank T-60A*

**DATA**
CREW  2
WEIGHT  9,960 kg  9.8 tons
HEIGHT  2.22 m  7 ft 3¼ in
LENGTH  5.00 m  16 ft 5 in
WIDTH  2.52 m  8 ft 3¼ in
ENGINE  2×ZIS-202 6-cyl. water-cooled petrol
developing 70 hp (each)
SPEED  Road 51 kmh  31.7 mph
Cross-country 30 kmh  18.6 mph
ROAD RADIUS  446 km  277 miles
ARMAMENT  One 45-mm gun and one 7.62-mm
DT mg
ROUNDS CARRIED  70×45 mm  945×7.62 mm
ARMOUR THICKNESS  Max 60 mm  2.36 in
Min 10 mm  .39 in

## *Lyokhy Tank T-70* (Light Tank T-70)

During January 1942 the T-70 light tank began to replace the earlier T-60 model. Despite the fact that it had been shown that the light tank was not an effective combat vehicle, it was cheaper and easier to mass-produce, which meant that units could receive tanks where they would otherwise have had none. The T-70 light tank was mass-produced at the Gorki Automobile Works, and had the same chassis as the T-60 (with the drive taken to the front instead of the rear), slightly reinforced to take the extra weight. A new turret was fitted mounting a 45-mm gun and co-axial 7.62-mm DT machine-gun. The hull armour was also modified to give a cleaner outline and better protection, and the driver was provided with an armoured visor. Performance was improved through the use of two engines in place of one. During 1943 an improved model, sometimes referred to as T-70A, appeared which had increased armour and slightly more powerful engines. Production of T-70 tanks was ceased in autumn 1943 after completion of 8,226 vehicles.

*Light Tank T-70A*

*Light Tank T-70A*

## Lyokhy Kolesogusenichny Bistrokhodny Tank BT (Light Wheel-track Fast Tank BT series)

Alongside the T-26 light tank, the BT fast tank was the most prolific armoured fighting vehicle, and the most popular, in the Red Army during the 1930s. The initials BT were an acronym for 'Bistrokhodny Tank', or Fast Tank. It was known among Soviet tankmen as the 'Betka' (Beetle) or as the 'Tri-Tankista' (Three Tank-men) as the result of its 3-man crew. The BT tank was derived from the American tank design by J. W. Christie, an example of which was purchased by Soviet officials in the US during 1930 and shipped back to the Kharkov Locomotive Works. After extensive development work the Revolutionary Military Council authorised the BT tank for adoption by the Red Army on 23 May 1931. Production work began at the 'Komintern' Works during August, and on 3 September the first two prototypes, designated BT-1, were delivered to the Red Army for trials. This first model was provided with machine-gun armament only, and it was requested that the production model be armed with an artillery weapon. In the meantime, the BT-2 model, still with only machine-gun armament was adopted in limited quantities. During production, successive BT-2 tanks were equipped with the 37-mm gun Model 1930. During 1932 the Red Army requested that the BT tank be armed with the more powerful 45-mm gun, and after a number of experimental trials the BT-5 was adopted with this gun mounted in a larger turret. Commanders' vehicles (BT-5U, BT-5TU) were provided with two-way radio equipment and had a frame aerial around the turret top. A special artillery support model was developed, designated BT-5A, mounting a short-barrelled 76.2-mm gun. Resulting from experience in combat (Spain and Manchuria) the Red Army requested that the BT be redesigned with sloped, welded armour. As the result the BT-7 model appeared. Command and artillery models were developed, with the same suffices as for the BT-5 model. During 1938 a new diesel engine had been developed for tank use, and this was installed in all subsequent BT-7 tanks, now referred to as BT-7M (also as BT-8). The Red Army also adopted a multiplicity of special purpose tanks based on these models (flame-throwers, bridge-layers, chemical tanks, etc).

---

DATA

**Model  BT-2**
CREW  3
WEIGHT  10,200 kg  10 tons
HEIGHT  2.38 m  7 ft 9½ in
LENGTH  5.90 m  19 ft 4¼ in
WIDTH  2.40 m  7 ft 10¼ in
ENGINE  Liberty aero 12-cyl. petrol developing 343 hp
SPEED  Road 110 kmh  68.4 mph
　　　　Cross-country 50 kmh  31 mph
ROAD RADIUS  300 km  186.4 miles
ARMAMENT  Two 7.62-mm mgs or one 37-mm M 1930 gun
ROUNDS CARRIED  4,000×7.62 mm
　　　　96×37 mm
ARMOUR THICKNESS  Max 13 mm  .51 in
　　　　Min  6 mm  .24 in

**Model  BT-5**
CREW  3
WEIGHT  11,500 kg  11.3 tons
HEIGHT  2.38 m  7 ft 9½ in
LENGTH  5.93 m  19 ft 5½ in
WIDTH  2.40 m  7 ft 10¼ in
ENGINE  M-5 aero 12-cyl. petrol developing 350 hp
SPEED  Road 110 kmh  68.4 mph
　　　　Cross-country 50 kmh  31 mph
ROAD RADIUS  300 km  186.4 miles
ARMAMENT  One 45-mm gun and one 7.62-mm mg
ROUNDS CARRIED  72-115×45 mm
　　　　2,394×7.62 mm
ARMOUR THICKNESS  Max 13 mm  .51 in
　　　　Min  6 mm  .24 in

**Model  BT-7**
CREW  3
WEIGHT  13,800 kg  13.6 tons
HEIGHT  2.62 m  8 ft 7 in
LENGTH  6.11 m  20 ft 0½ in
WIDTH  2.62 m  8 ft 7 in
ENGINE  M-17T 12-cyl. petrol developing 450 hp
SPEED  Road 74 kmh  46 mph
　　　　Cross-country 50 kmh  31 mph
ROAD RADIUS  500 km  311 miles
ARMAMENT  One 45-mm gun and one 7.62-mm mg
ROUNDS CARRIED  132-188×45 mm
　　　　2,394×7.62 mm
ARMOUR THICKNESS  Max 22 mm  .87 in
　　　　Min  6 mm  .24 in

**Model  BT-7M**
CREW  3
WEIGHT  14,650 kg  14.4 tons
HEIGHT  2.46 m  8 ft 0½ in
LENGTH  6.11 m  20 ft 0½ in
WIDTH  2.62 m  8 ft 7 in
ENGINE  V-2 12-cyl. diesel developing 500 hp
SPEED  Road 86 kmh  53.4 mph
　　　　Cross-country 50 kmh  31 mph
ROAD RADIUS  700 km  435 miles
ARMAMENT  One 76.2-mm gun and two 7.62-mm mgs
ROUNDS CARRIED  40×76.2 mm
　　　　2,394×7.62 mm
ARMOUR THICKNESS  Max 22 mm  .87 in
　　　　Min  6 mm  .24 in

*Fast Tank BT-2 with 37-mm gun* ▲

▼ *Fast Tank BT-5*

*Fast Tank BT-5U Commanders' model*

*Fast Tank BT-7*

## *Sredny Tank T-28* (Medium Tank T-28)

In 1932 the Leningrad Kirov Tank Plant built a new prototype medium tank based on the general design of the British A-6E1 16-ton tank. The first Soviet specification for a multi-turreted 16-ton medium tank, intended for breaking through strongly-fortified defensive zones and for exploitation by mechanised units, was issued to the Kirov plant in 1931. After trials with the prototype heavier armour and more powerful armament were requested, the original 45-mm gun being replaced by a 76.2-mm gun. A specification was then drafted for a 28-ton medium tank, designated T-28. The final model was accepted for adoption by the Red Army on 11 August 1933. In later production models a turret stabilisation system was utilised. During 1938 this tank was subjected to extensive modification, resulting in the T-28 Ob.1938. The existing 16.5 calibre gun was replaced by the L-10 gun of 26 calibres. During the Russo-Finnish War (1939-40) it was discovered that the armour was inadequate and so the vehicle was up-armoured by the use of 'screened armour'. The turret and hull front plates were increased from 50 to 80-mm, the sides and rear to 40-mm. The weight of the new tank rose to 32 tons.

**DATA**
CREW  6
WEIGHT  28,000 kg   27.6 tons
HEIGHT  2.82 m   9 ft 3 in
LENGTH  7.44 m   24 ft 5 in
WIDTH  2.81 m   9 ft 2¼ in
ENGINE  M-17L 12-cyl. water-cooled petrol
    developing 500 hp
SPEED  Road 37 kmh   23 mph

Cross-country 20 kmh   12.4 mph
ROAD RADIUS  220 km   137 miles
ARMAMENT  One 76.2-mm gun and three 7.62-mm
    DT mgs
ROUNDS CARRIED  70×76.2 mm
    7,938×7.62 mm
ARMOUR THICKNESS  Max 80 mm   3.15 in
    Min 20 mm   .79 in

*Medium Tank T-28*

*T-28 late production model*

### *Sredny Tank T-34* (Medium Tank T-34 series)

At the beginning of 1937 the Komintern Factory in Khar'kov was assigned the task of developing a new medium tank with shell-proof armour. Several experimental vehicles were designed and built under the guidance of Chief Designer M.I. Koshkin, which were essentially outgrowths of the BT (Christie) wheel/track series. These culminated in a final wheel/track model designated T-32. In the meantime, Koshkin had proposed that a new medium tank be developed which ran on tracks only, and this was sanctioned. The two prototypes (the tracked variant being called T-34) were subjected to rigorous trials, and the T-34 model finally accepted as the standard medium tank for the Red Army on 19 December, 1939. Towards the end of 1940 the first production models of the T-34, designated T-34 Ob.1940 (often referred to as T-34A), were released from the Komintern Factory. During 1940 115 T-34s were produced, and some of these were despatched to Finland for combat tests but arrived too late to participate in operations. By 22 June 1941—when the Germans attacked—a total of 1,225 had been produced. By the time of the Battle of Moscow (December 5th, 1941) 1,853 had been delivered to the Red Army, but of course many of these had since been destroyed. The T-34 made its debut on 22 June 1941 in the vicinity of Grodno (Belorussia). It was a complete surprise to the German High Command, who learned to treat this tank with the greatest respect. There were many design and production changes made to the T-34 during its production but there is obviously insufficient room here to go into detail. The first fundamental change was to re-arm the tank with the longer-barrelled Model 40 F-34 gun (in place of the original L-11 gun). Only modification to the armour and automotive layout ensued until autumn 1943, when the 85-mm gun was fitted in a new, enlarged turret. This final model was designated T-34-85. The T-34-85 was approved for adoption by the Red Army on December 15th 1943. Over 40,000 T-34s were manufactured until the end of the war.

*Medium Tank T-34 1940 model* ▲

*T-34 with cast turret that also appeared in 1943*

*T-34 1941 model* ▶ ▲

*T-34 1943 model* ▶ ▼

DATA

| Model | T-34 Ob.1940 | | Model | T-34-85 Ob.1943 |
|---|---|---|---|---|
| CREW | 4 | | CREW | 5 |
| WEIGHT | 26,300 kg  25.9 tons | | WEIGHT | 31,500 kg  31 tons |
| HEIGHT | 2.45 m  8 ft 0½ in | | HEIGHT | 2.56 m  8 ft 5 in |
| LENGTH | 5.92 m  19 ft 5¼ in | | LENGTH | 8.07 m  26 ft 5¾ in (incl. gun) |
| | | | | 5.92 m  19 ft 5¼ in (less gun) |
| WIDTH | 3.00 m  9 ft 10 in | | WIDTH | 3.21 m  10 ft 6¼ in |
| ENGINE | V-2-34 12-cyl. water-cooled diesel developing 500 hp | | | |
| SPEED | Road 54 kmh  34 mph | | SPEED | 50 kmh  31 mph |
| | Cross-country  40 kmh  25 mph | | | Cross-country  35 kmh  21.8 mph |
| ROAD RADIUS | 400 km  248.6 miles | | ROAD RADIUS | 300 km  186.4 miles |
| ARMAMENT | One 76.2-mm L-11 gun and | | ARMAMENT | One 85-mm ZIS S-53 gun and two |
| | two 7.62-mm DT mgs | | | 7.62-mm DT mgs |
| ROUNDS CARRIED | 77×76.2 mm | | ROUNDS CARRIED | 55×85 mm |
| | 4,725×7.62 mm | | | 2,394×7.62 mm |
| ARMOUR THICKNESS | Max 45 mm  1.77 in | | ARMOUR THICKNESS | Max 60 mm  2.36 in |
| | Min 16 mm  .63 in | | | Min 18 mm  .71 in |

*T-34/85*

## *Sredny Tank T-43* (Medium Tank T-43)

During 1943 a small number of T-34 tanks were produced with much thicker armour. These were designated T-43. Since they still retained the original 76.2-mm gun, however, they were not very successful and were soon replaced in service by the T-34-85 tank with the powerful 85-mm gun.

DATA

| | | | | |
|---|---|---|---|---|
| CREW | 4 | | | |
| WEIGHT | 31,000 kg  30.5 tons | | ROAD RADIUS | 400 km  248.6 miles |
| HEIGHT | 2.79 m  9 ft 2 in | | ARMAMENT | One 76.2-mm gun and two 7.62-mm |
| LENGTH | 7.38 m  24 ft 2½ in | | | DT mgs |
| WIDTH | 3.21 m  10 ft 6¼ in | | ROUNDS CARRIED | 77×76.2 mm |
| ENGINE | V-2-34 12-cyl. diesel developing 500 hp | | | 2,394×7.62 mm |
| SPEED | Road 50 kmh  31 mph | | ARMOUR THICKNESS | Max 110 mm  4.33 in |
| | Cross-country 40 kmh  25 mph | | | Min  22 mm  .87 in |

*Medium Tank T-43*

DATA
CREW  4
WEIGHT   31,900 kg   31.4 tons
HEIGHT   2.57 m   8 ft 5½ in
LENGTH   8.23 m   27 ft 0 in
WIDTH   3.34 m   10 ft 11½ in
ENGINE   V-2-44 12-cyl. water-cooled diesel
           developing 512 hp
SPEED   Road 51 kmh   32 mph
         Cross-country 40 kmh   25 mph
ROAD RADIUS   300 km   186.4 miles
ARMAMENT   One 85-mm ZIS S-53 gun and three
           7.62-mm DT mgs
ROUNDS CARRIED   58×85 mm   1,890×7.62 mm
ARMOUR THICKNESS   Max 120 mm   4.72 in
                  Min   15 mm   .59 in

## *Sredny Tank T-44* (Medium Tank T-44)

During 1944 a new medium tank was built on the basis of the T-34-85, and designated T-44. Due to the hurried development work this vehicle was not very successful. The first production model mounted an 85-mm gun and saw limited action in early 1945. Technologically, there was substantial changes in comparison with the T-34 model, particularly the transversely mounted engine and the use of torsion-bar suspension.

*Medium Tank T-44*

## *Tyazholy Tank T-35* (Heavy Tank T-35 series)

At the beginning of the 1930s the Red Army Staff envisaged vehicles of the heavy, multi-turreted type for operating as a shock-force when breaking through enemy defensive positions. Based on the general philosophy of the British A-1 'Independent' Tank (a specimen was never actually purchased), the 37-ton prototype of the T-35 was built. The vehicle had five turrets—a main one mounting a 76.2-mm gun, two diagonally-placed subsidiary turrets each mounting one 37-mm gun (front and rear of the main turret), and two further small turrets each with one 7.62-mm machine-gun. Subsequent production vehicles dispensed with some of these turrets, and a few had 45-mm guns in place of the 37-mm type. The final model had sloping welded armour. Even though the T-35 was outmoded

DATA

CREW   11 (when all turrets fitted)

WEIGHT   50,000 kg   49.2 tons

HEIGHT   3.43 m   11 ft 3 in

LENGTH   9.72 m   31 ft 10 in

WIDTH   3.20 m   10 ft 6 in

ENGINE   M-17T 12 cyl. water-cooled petrol
developing 500 hp

SPEED   Road 30 kmh   18.6 mph
Cross-country 20 kmh   12.4 mph

ROAD RADIUS   150 km   93.2 miles

ARMAMENT   One 76.2-mm gun, two 45-mm guns,
six DT machine-guns, one P-40 AA
machine-gun (some later models had
some of the subsidiary weapons
removed)

ROUNDS CARRIED   90×76.2 mm   226×45
mm   10,000×7.62 mm

ARMOUR THICKNESS   Max 30 mm   1.18 in
Min 10 mm   .39 in

by the beginning of the Russo-German War, it was retained in service until its final action during the Battle for Moscow (December 1941). The T-35 appeared in several variants and about 60 were produced and issued to the tank brigades of the High Command Reserve.

*Heavy Tank T-35*

*Heavy Tank T-35. On this vehicle the right auxiliary turret is armed with a 45-mm gun*

## *Tyazholy Tank KV* (Heavy Tank 'Klim Voroshilov' series)

At the outbreak of World War II the Soviet Army was practically the only armed force in the World to be equipped with production heavy tanks. The first of these, the KV-1 ('Klim Voroshilov') was designed by the group of engineers at the Kirov Factory in Leningrad, under the direction of Zh. Kotin. Work on the new tank began in February 1939 and the State Defence Committee approved a mock-up in April. The completed tank was demonstrated to the Red Army Staff in September. It was accepted as standard at the same time as the T-34 medium, on 19 December 1939. Production began in February 1940 and 243 vehicles were produced by the

*KV-1s line up in forest ready to advance* ▶

DATA
**Model KV-1**
CREW 5
WEIGHT 46,350 kg 45.6 tons
HEIGHT 2.87 m 9 ft 5½ in
LENGTH 7.41 m 24 ft 3½ in
WIDTH 3.49 m 11 ft 5½ in
ENGINE V-2K 12-cyl. water-cooled
    diesel developing 550 hp
SPEED Road 35 kmh 21.8 mph
    Cross-country 20 kmh 12.4 mph
ROAD RADIUS 225 km 140 miles
ARMAMENT One 76.2-mm M 1938/39 gun
    and three 7.62-mm mgs
ROUNDS CARRIED 111×76.2 mm
    3,024×7.62 mm
ARMOUR THICKNESS Max 106 mm 4.17 in
    Min 30 mm 1.18 in

end of the year. A platoon of KVs was sent to Finland for combat tests, and in February 1940 they took part in the break-through of the Finnish positions. Despite innumerable hits from Finnish anti-tank guns, not one of the vehicles was put out of action. Subsequent production was undertaken at the Chelyabinsk Tractor Factory. By 22 June 1941 a total of 636 had been built, and by the time of the Battle for Moscow—1,364. Throughout the war some 13,500 vehicles (tanks and self-propelled guns) were turned out on the KV chassis. Alongside the KV-1 (76.2-mm gun), a special artillery fire-support version was adopted mounting a 152-mm howitzer in a rotating turret. This was designated KV-2, but due to poor performance the vehicle was removed from production. As in the case of the T-34, several models of the KV were developed, but the two most significant were the KV-1s and the KV-85. The KV-1s was a lightened version with less armour—enabling it to move faster. It was not long, however, before the Soviets returned to the up-armoured version. Towards the end of its life, in autumn 1943, work was being carried out on the new IS heavy tank and the original turret—mounting an 85-mm gun—was retrofitted to the KV chassis as an expedient pending final introduction of the new tank. This final KV model was designated KV-85.

DATA

| **Model KV-1s** | **Model KV-2** | **Model KV-85** |
|---|---|---|
| CREW 5 | CREW 6 | CREW 4 |
| WEIGHT 42,500 kg 41.8 tons | WEIGHT 53,000 kg 52.2 tons | WEIGHT 46,000 kg 45.3 tons |
| HEIGHT 3.21 m 10 ft 6½ in | HEIGHT 3.93 m 12 ft 11 in | HEIGHT 3.11 m 10 ft 2½ in |
| LENGTH 7.25 m 23 ft 9½ in | LENGTH 7.31 m 23 ft 11¾ in | LENGTH 9.13 m 29 ft 11½ in |
| WIDTH 3.51 m 11 ft 6½ in | WIDTH 3.58 m 11 ft 9 in | WIDTH 3.50 m 11 ft 5¾ in |
| ENGINE V-2K-s 12-cyl. water-cooled diesel developing 600 hp | ENGINE V-2K 12-cyl. water-cooled diesel developing 550 hp | ENGINE V-2K-s 12-cyl. water-cooled diesel developing 600 hp |
| SPEED Road 40 kmh 25 mph Cross-country 25 kmh 15.5 mph | SPEED Road 26 kmh 16.2 mph Cross-country 15 kmh 9.3 mph | SPEED Road 35 kmh 21.8 mph Cross-country 20 kmh 12.4 mph |
| ROAD RADIUS 250 km 155.3 miles | ROAD RADIUS 160 km 99.4 miles | ROAD RADIUS 225 km 140 miles |
| ARMAMENT One 76.2-mm M 1940 gun and three 7.62-mm mgs | ARMAMENT One 152-mm M 1938/40 howitzer and two mgs | ARMAMENT One 85-mm M 1943 gun and three 7.62-mm mgs |
| ROUNDS CARRIED 102×76.2 mm 3,042×7.62 mm | ROUNDS CARRIED 36×152 mm 3,078×7.62 mm | ROUNDS CARRIED 71×85 mm 3,276×7.62 mm |
| ARMOUR THICKNESS Max 82 mm 3.23 in Min 30 mm 1.18 in | ARMOUR THICKNESS Max 110 mm 4.33 in Min 35 mm 1.38 in | ARMOUR THICKNESS Max 110 mm 4.33 in Min 30 mm 1.18 in |

*Heavy Tank KV-1*

*KV-2 showing the massive turret and 152-mm gun*

*View of KV-2 with gun pointing to the rear*

*KV-85*

## *Tyazholy Tank IS* (Heavy Tank 'Iosef Stalin' series)

In August 1942 the Soviet High Command requested the development of a new heavy tank that would prove capable of defeating any future types likely to be introduced by the enemy. Work on the new project was undertaken by a special design group, called the 'IS Bureau', under the leadership of Zh. Kotin. Based on experiments with prototype KV models (KV-3 and KV-13) in 1943 the design bureau investigated a new project designated IS ('Iosef Stalin'). Early in autumn 1943 the first three prototypes of the IS-1 (also called IS-85 due to its 85-mm armament) were completed, tested and finally approved. Directions to begin mass-production were issued in October 1943. Soon after the start of production, the need arose for more powerful armament, and a few prototypes were tested with a new 100-mm gun (IS-100). A design group under General Petrov, however, conceived a scheme for mounting a 122-mm gun, which was accepted. On 31 October 1943 the new model, designated IS-2 (IS-122), was accepted as standard; by the end of the year the Kirov Factory had produced 102 of this new model. The IS tank was used for the first time during February 1944 at Korsun Shevcherkov. After producing several more experimental vehicles of this type, work on further improvement to the armour layout led to the IS-3 model towards the end of 1944. With its greatly contoured armour this new heavy tank caused a sensation throughout the world which lasted well into the 1950s.

┌─ DATA ─────────────────────────────────────────────────────────────────────────────────────────────

**Model IS-1**
CREW 4
WEIGHT 44,000 kg 43.3 tons
HEIGHT 2.92 m 9 ft 6½ in
LENGTH 8.95 m 29 ft 4 in
WIDTH 3.36 m 11 ft
ENGINE V-2-IS (V-2K) 12-cyl. water-cooled diesel developing 513 hp
SPEED Road 37 kmh 23 mph
        Cross-country 24 kmh 15 mph
ROAD RADIUS 240 km 149 miles
ARMAMENT One 85-mm M1943 gun and
        three 7.62-mm mgs
ROUNDS CARRIED 71×85 mm
        1,330×7.62 mm
ARMOUR THICKNESS Max 120 mm 4.72 in
        Min 25 mm .98 in

**Model IS-2**
CREW 4
WEIGHT 45,000 kg 44.3 tons
HEIGHT 2.92 m 9 ft 6½ in
LENGTH 10.33 m 33 ft 10¾ in
WIDTH 3.36 m 11 ft

SPEED Road 37 kmh 23 mph
        Cross-country 24 kmh 15 mph
ROAD RADIUS 240 km 149 miles
ARMAMENT One 122-mm M1943 gun, one 12.7-mm
        AA, and three 7.62-mm mgs
ROUNDS CARRIED 28×122 mm
        2,330×7.62 mm
ARMOUR THICKNESS Max 120 mm 4.72 in
        Min 25 mm .98 in

**Model IS-3**
CREW 4
WEIGHT 45,800 kg 45 tons
HEIGHT 2.92 m 9 ft 6½ in
LENGTH 10.74 m 35 ft 3 in
WIDTH 3.44 m 11 ft 3½ in

SPEED Road 37 kmh 23 mph
        Cross-country 24 kmh 15 mph
ROAD RADIUS 208 km 129.3 miles
ARMAMENT One 122-mm M1943 gun, one 12.7-mm
        AA, and one/two 7.62-mm mgs
ROUNDS CARRIED 28×122 mm
        1,000×7.62 mm
ARMOUR THICKNESS Max 230 mm 9.06 in
        Min 25 mm .98 in

└────────────────────────────────────────────────────────────────────────────────────────────────────

*IS-2 carrying infantrymen on the outskirts of Berlin*

▲ *IS-2 advance in East Prussia*                    *IS-3 showing the improved armour layout* ▼

# UNITED STATES

## Introduction

American tank development between the two world wars was almost moribund in comparison with other major nations. An adequate stock of tanks built in 1919-20 was available but the Tank Corps had been abolished in 1920 leaving tanks as an infantry commitment. J. Walter Christie, an ingenious but sometimes erratic engineer, produced some brilliant and advanced fast tank designs, though few interested the US Army or saw service. When General MacArthur became Army Chief of Staff in 1932 he instituted a mechanisation programme which led to the design of a simple but sturdy light tank (the T2) which was developed as a light tank for the infantry and a combat car for the cavalry. The basic design of these vehicles was followed by the whole series of M3 and M5 light tanks which appeared in World War II. In the area of medium tanks, a new standard design, the T5, was produced by Rock Island Arsenal in 1938 and this was developed into the M2 and M2A1 medium tanks of 1939-40. In the meantime the war had begun in Europe and it was apparent that the US Army was woefully under-equipped for waging war. In 1940 a new Armored Force command was set up. It had been realised earlier that government arsenals could not possibly build tanks in quantities envisaged for a nation at war. Contingency plans were made to place production orders with heavy engineering plants, but in the event it was the automobile industry which was harnessed to turn out tanks in the quantities the army needed. Such firms as Chrysler, Fisher, General Motors and Ford, working in conjunction with the Ordnance Dept, built the bulk of American AFVs in the 1940-45 period with remarkable efficiency and speed. Observing the results of the early months of the war in Europe the army was able to get into production a medium tank (M3) with 75-mm gun, closely followed by the superior M4 (Sherman) with same basic armament. This tank formed the backbone of the armoured forces from 1942 to 1945. It proved so reliable that the US Army delayed getting heavier tanks into service until it was almost too late. However, an efficient, if not brilliant heavy tank, M26 (Pershing), with 90-mm gun was in service in the closing months of the war as an answer to heavy German types like the 'Tiger' and 'Royal Tiger' which had superior firepower to all other US tanks. In general American tanks were very effective in World War II. They carried big guns and were big enough to be upgunned. They were mechanically reliable, rugged and simple to maintain. And above all, they were available in huge numbers, sufficient to give America and her Allies complete domination of any battlefield in the last two years of the war.

---

## Light Tank M2A4

At the opening of World War II the standard light tank of the United States Army was the M2A4. Standardised in 1939, this vehicle went into production in June 1940, and was the culmination of light tank development begun in 1935. Armed with a 37-mm gun and a co-axial .30 cal. Browning machine-gun, it also carried four additional .30 cal mgs, mounted two in side sponsons, one in the hull front and one in a anti-aircraft mount outside the turret. The M2A4 saw service in the early Pacific campaigns, but most of them were used for training. A small batch of these tanks were delivered to the British in 1941, but these also were used only for training.

DATA
CREW 4
WEIGHT 11,480 kg   11.3 tons
HEIGHT 2.49 m   8 ft 2 in
LENGTH 4.42 m   14 ft 6 in
WIDTH 2.47 m   8 ft 1¼ in
ENGINE Continental W-670 developing 250 hp
SPEED Road 40 kmh   25 mph
Cross-country 29 kmh   18 mph
ROAD RADIUS 209 km   130 miles
ARMAMENT One 37-mm gun and five .30 cal
(7.62-mm) Browning mgs
ROUNDS CARRIED 107×37 mm   7,185×7.62 mm
ARMOUR THICKNESS Max 25 mm   .98 in
Min 6 mm   .24 in

*Light Tank M2A4 of the Marine Corps in action on Guadalcanal Island*

## Light Tank M3

DATA
CREW  4
WEIGHT  13,680 kg  13.46 tons
HEIGHT  2.51 m  8 ft 3 in
LENGTH  4.54 m  14 ft 10½ in
WIDTH  2.24 m  7 ft 4 in
ENGINE  Continental W-670 developing 250 hp
SPEED  Road 58 kmh  36 mph
　　　　Cross-country 32 kmh  20 mph
ROAD RADIUS  113 km  70 miles
ARMAMENT  One 37-mm gun and five .30 cal
　　　　　　(7.62-mm) Browning mgs
ROUNDS CARRIED  103×37 mm  8,270×7.62 mm
ARMOUR THICKNESS  Max 51 mm  2.00 in
　　　　　　　　　Min 10 mm  .39 in

*M3 light tanks with welded turrets in service with the British Army in the desert. (Stuart Is)*

Based on the Light Tank M2A4 and equipped with the same armament, the M3 was fitted with heavier armour and incorporated various improvements. Standardised in July 1940, this vehicle went into production in March 1941 and was supplied to the Allies, under Lend-Lease, as well as to the American Forces through 1941 and 1942. Designated General Stuart (Stuart I) by the British Army and nicknamed 'Honey' by the British troops, these tanks won high praise during the Libyan Campaign.

Numerous improvements were made throughout the production period, so that the final M3s were vastly different to the first versions. The early models were entirely riveted with a seven-sided turret. Later a welded seven-sided turret was used, and still later, a rounded, welded homogeneous turret was installed. The final models were entirely welded. A gyrostabiliser to permit accurate firing of the 37-mm gun while the tank was in motion, was incorporated in late 1941. As a result of battle experience in North Africa, additional fuel capacity was provided by two jettison fuel tanks. 500 Light Tank M3s were fitted with the Guiberson T.1020 Diesel engine; this variant was known to the British as the Stuart II.

## Light Tank M3A1

DATA
WEIGHT  14,220 kg  14 tons
HEIGHT  2.30 m  7 ft 6½ in
ROUNDS CARRIED  116 × 37 mm
　　　　　　　　6,400 × 7.62 mm
Other data as for Light Tank M3.

This was a further improved model that was standardised in August 1941. The turret was similar to that of the final version of the Light Tank M3, but the cupola was eliminated to reduce the overall height. The fighting compartment was now integrated with the turret, and was rotated with it, either by a hydraulic mechanism or by hand. An improved gun mount for the turret had a periscope sight, and an additional periscope was provided in the turret roof. Other armament was the same as that on the Light Tank M3, except that the sponson machine-guns were omitted. This version saw service in China, Burma, and India. British designation for this version was Stuart III.

*M3A1 light tank of Marine Corps moving ashore on the Japanese-held island of Emirau in the Bismarck Archipelago*

# Light Tank M3A3

This was the final production variant and was standardised in August 1942 as a modification of Light Tank M3A1 The driver's compartment was enlarged, the hatches being moved to the top plate; the sponsons were redesigned, elimination of the sponson guns providing space for two additional fuel tanks, engine air cleaners and more room for ammunition stowage.

The turret was redesigned with a bulge at the rear to provide space for a radio set. Sand shields were fitted over the suspension. British designation was Stuart V. In action in North Africa, the Soviet Union and Burma.

*M3A3 light tank manned by Chinese crew operating in Northern Burma 1944*

# Light Tank M5

This vehicle was designed to use twin Cadillac engines with Hydromatic transmission, providing automatic gear shifting. The hull was fabricated of welded homogeneous armour plate, with reinforced front plate and extended sponsons. Elimination of bolts and rivets reduced the danger of these parts being driven inside the vehicle if the tank received a hit. This streamlined effect was subsequently adopted for the Light Tank M3A3. To accommodate the twin Cadillac engines, the rear engine covers were stepped-up. The welded, power-operated turret and integrated turret basket was similar to that of the Light Tank M3A3, and a gyrostabiliser was fitted for the 37-mm gun. Standardised in February 1942, this vehicle saw action in Tunisia with the US Forces, in Italy with the British Forces, Normandy 1944-45 and on the Eastern Front 1944-45. British designation, Stuart VI.

*M5 Light Tanks, followed by American infantrymen move through the jungle forests of the Arawe Peninsula in New Britain*

# Light Tank M5A1

Standardised in September 1942, this vehicle replaced Light Tank M5 in production. Principal change was in the use of an improved turret with a radio bulge at the rear, similar to the turret of the Light Tank M3A3. The improved turret provided more room for the turret crew; a radio antenna bracket was mounted above the bulge. The anti-aircraft mount was relocated, and larger escape hatches were provided. First used in action during the Casablanca landings in 1942; also saw service in Western Europe.

**DATA**
CREW 4
WEIGHT 16,920 kg 16.65 tons
HEIGHT 2.17 m 7 ft 10½ in
LENGTH 4.84 m 15 ft 10½ in
WIDTH 2.29 m 7 ft 6 in
ROUNDS CARRIED 147 × 37 mm
6,500 × 7.62 mm

*Light Tank M5A1 of the US 12th Armored Division moving through the German town of Neustadt*

# Light Tank M22 (Airborne)

Light Tank M22 was designed to provide support firepower in a vehicle light enough to be carried by airplane. Four brackets, located above and to the rear of the bogie suspension, were provided for attaching the tank between the landing gear of a C-54 transport plane, the fighting compartment and turret being removable for this purpose. Armament consisted of one 37-mm gun and a co-axial .30-cal machine-gun. Because of weight limitations, no power-traverse, gyro-stabiliser or hull machine-gun were fitted. Production of the M22 was begun in March 1943, but this tank was never used by American troops in combat. A number were supplied to the British under Lend-Lease for airborne operations. Known as the Locust, about 15 were carried inside Hamilcar gliders during the Rhine crossing by the British 6th Airborne Division on 24 March 1945

**DATA**
CREW 3
WEIGHT 8,180 kg 8.05 tons
HEIGHT 1.85 m 6 ft 1 in
LENGTH 3.94 m 12 ft 11 in
WIDTH 2.16 m 7 ft 1 in
ENGINE Lycoming 0-435T developing 162 hp
SPEED Road 64.4 kmh 40 mph
Cross-country 48.3 kmh 30 mph
ROAD RADIUS 217 km 135 miles
ARMAMENT One 37-mm gun and one .30-cal mg
ROUNDS CARRIED 50 × 37mm
2,500 × 7.62 mm
ARMOUR THICKNESS Max 25 mm .98 in
Min 9 mm .35 in

*Light airborne tank 'Locust' of the British Airborne Division leaving Hamilcar glider*

DATA

CREW  4

WEIGHT  19,330 kg   19.03 tons

HEIGHT  2.46 m   8 ft 1 in

LENGTH  4.95 m   16 ft 3 in

WIDTH  2.84 m   9 ft 4 in

ENGINE  Twin Cadillac V-8 developing 220 hp

SPEED  Road  56 kmh   35 mph

Cross-country  40 kmh   25 mph

ROAD RADIUS  161 km   100 miles

ARMAMENT  One 75-mm gun, three 0.30-cal
(7.62-mm) and one 0.50-cal (12.7-mm)
mgs

ROUNDS CARRIED  48×75 mm
440×12.7 mm
3,750×7.62 mm

ARMOUR THICKNESS  Max 25 mm   .98 in
Min  9 mm   .35 in

*Light Tank M24 General Chaffe*

DATA

CREW  6

WEIGHT  29,930 kg   29.46 tons

HEIGHT  3.12 m   10 ft 3 in

LENGTH  5.64 m   18 ft 6 in

WIDTH  2.72 m   8 ft 11 in

ENGINE  Continental R-975-EC2 developing 340 hp

SPEED  Road  42 kmh   26 mph

Cross-country  25.8 kmh   16 mph

ROAD RADIUS  193 km   120 miles

ARMAMENT  One 75-mm gun and three or four
0.30-cal (7.62-mm) mgs

ROUNDS CARRIED  46×75 mm
178×37 mm
9,200×7.62 mm

ARMOUR THICKNESS  Max 37 mm   1.46 in
Min 12 mm   .47 in

## Light Tank M24 General Chaffe

Standardised in July 1944, the M24 was the last American light tank to be produced in World War II. This vehicle was developed to provide a light tank with improved flotation, mobility and increased firepower. Incorporating a 75-mm M6 gun with concentric recoil mechanism, an Ordnance refinement of an aircraft cannon, the M24 was also equipped with improved fire control in the form of gun elevation stabiliser and a power-operated turret. There was no turret basket; seats for the turret crew were suspended from the base ring. A .50-cal machine-gun was pintle-mounted at the rear of the turret for anti-aircraft protection, and two .30-cal machine-guns were carried, one in the hull front, and one as a co-axial with the 75-mm gun. A 2-inch mortar was mounted in the right front turret. Torsion bar suspension employed in conjunction with large rubber tyred wheels resulted in greater mobility. Wherever possible, unit assemblies were made so that they could be easily removed and rapidly replaced in the field.

Power was supplied by two 8-cylinder V-type liquid-cooled Cadillac engines through two Hydromatic transmissions.

The General Chaffe was used operationally in Europe and the Pacific.

## Medium Tank M3 General Grant (General Lee)

The medium tank in service with the American Army at the outbreak of the war was the M2A1, armed with a 37-mm gun and weighing 23 tons (23,370 kg). Although recently standardised, European battle experience was soon to show that this vehicle was tactically and technically obsolete. At a meeting in August 1940, the characteristics of a new medium tank were agreed upon. Basically, it was to be a vehicle with heavier armour and mounting a 75-mm gun. It was proposed and agreed that the 75-mm gun would be turret-mounted, but as insufficient development work had been done on the problem of mounting a gun of this weight, and the design of such a gun mount would require time, it was decided that the projected medium tank would mount the 75-mm gun in the right sponson. Experimental work on this type of gun mount had been done in 1938; the turret mounting of the gun would follow later.

By August 1941, full-scale production of the resulting vehicle, the M3, had started. The new tank was armed with the 75-mm M2 gun (M3 in later models) in the right sponson, one 37-mm gun and one .30-cal in the turret, one .30-cal machine-gun in the turret cupola and a .30-cal machine-gun in the hull front. The turret and sponson were cast and the hull of riveted construction. This was the first of the American tanks to employ gyrostabilisers and power-traversed turrets with integral fighting compartments. Combat experience in Africa and the Soviet Union suggested improvements, some of which were introduced during production; most of these improvements, however, were incorporated in the design of the Medium Tank M4. The British purchasing mission did not want the turret of the original M3 and through Lend-Lease had a special turret made that had space for a radio. Vehicles equipped with the British-designed turret were known as the General Grant. 200 of these tanks were shipped to the Middle East in time for the battle of Gazala and the retreat to El Alamein. In the summer of 1942, at the urgent British request for more tanks, the original M3s were withdrawn from US Armored Divisions and sent to Egypt; these were called General Lee tanks by the

British. The M3 series of medium tanks saw service in the Middle East, North Africa, the Soviet Union and Burma.

*M3 Medium Tank General Lee in service with the British Army in the Western Desert*

*M3 Medium Tank General Grant in action in the Western Desert*

## Medium Tank M3A1 (Lee II)

This was similar to Medium Tank M3 (Lee I), but had a cast upper hull. Side doors were later eliminated to strengthen the structure and an escape door placed in hull floor.

*M3A1 Medium Tank; cast hull and M2 75-mm gun with counter weight*

### Medium Tank M3A2 (Lee III)

This was mechanically identical to the M3 but had an all-welded hull.

### Medium Tank M3A3 (Lee V)

All-welded hull as M3A2, but was fitted with twin General Motors 6-71 Diesel engines of 375 hp. Weight now increased to 30.94 tons; top speed 46 kmh (29 mph). Side doors welded up or eliminated on late production models. Lee IV designation given by the British to the M3A3 vehicles fitted with the Continental engine.

### Medium Tank M3A4 (Lee VI)

*M3A4 Medium Tanks, with side doors eliminated and M3 75-mm gun*

Identical to M3, but now fitted with a Chrysler A-57 multi-bank 370 hp engine. This was made up of 5 automobile engines coupled together on a common drive shaft. Weight was increased to 31.43 tons, and the hull lengthened by 0.38 m to 6.45 m overall to accommodate the longer engine. Side doors were eliminated.

### Medium Tank M3A5 (Grant II)

As for M3A3, but with riveted instead of welded hull. Side doors welded-up or eliminated on late production vehicles of this series. All late production vehicles, irrespective of model, had the longer 75-mm M3 gun.

### Medium Tank M4 General Sherman

With the M3 Medium Tank design completed in March 1941, the Ordnance Department began work on its replacement. By April, five provisional schemes were shown to the Armored Board who selected the simplest for development.

Designated Medium Tank T6 after various modifications, this was standardised as the Medium Tank M4 in October 1941 and plans were made to put the M4 into production in early 1942 with a phased replacement of the M3 series vehicles on the various assembly lines then in operation. The M4 introduced a number of improvements over the M3 series, which they replaced in production. The silhouette was lowered by elimination of the cupola; this also resulted in a lower centre of gravity, making the M4 more stable. The 75-mm M3 gun with a co-axial .30-cal Browning machine-gun was located in a turret providing 360° traverse and greater elevation and depression than was possible in the Medium Tank M3. Other armament included a .30-cal machine-gun in the bow, a .50-cal machine-gun mounted on top of the turret for anti-aircraft defence, and a 2-inch smoke mortar. Indirect vision was provided for each member of the crew by means of periscopes. The vehicle was also equipped with a two-way radio and an interphone system.

A number of changes were made during production, with the result that later vehicles differed somewhat from those produced earlier.

The lower front plate of the hull on early models consisted of three pieces bolted together. Later production vehicles used a one-piece plate. Late production vehicles were fitted with Combination Gun Mount M34A1; this mount protected the co-axial machine-gun and telescope, as well as the 75-mm gun (the early Combination Gun Mount M34 had a front shield that protected the 75-mm gun only). Some vehicles had a track-supporting roller directly over the suspension bracket, others had the roller offset to the rear of the bracket. The M4 Medium Tank series was the most widely produced, most widely used, and the most important of all tanks in service with the British, American and Allied Forces in World War II. From late 1944, M4 vehicles in production were fitted with the new horizontal volute spring suspension in place of the vertical volute type. The HVSS was designed to give improved flotation and simpler maintenance; track width of the new suspension was increased from the original $16\frac{1}{2}$ in (0.42 m) to 23 in (0.58 m). Vehicles equipped with the new suspension were known as M4A3 (76-mm) HVSS, M4A2 (76-mm) HVSS and M4A1 (76-mm) HVSS. A small number of these tanks were taken into British service and received the suffix Y (Sherman IIAY, Sherman IIIAY). The M4 first saw action with the British at El Alamein and thereafter served in nearly all theatres of war, including the Eastern Front.

## Medium Tank M4

This was the original design with Continental engine, but with a simplified all-welded hull instead of the cast hull initially devised. Early vehicles had a three-piece bolted nose and the narrow M34 gun mount. Later vehicles had a one-piece cast nose and the wide M34A1 gun mount. This was the third of the series to go into production. British designation for the M4 was Sherman I.

*Medium Tank M4*

*Medium Tank M4. Late production model with one-piece cast nose on the Philippine Island of Leyte*

*M4A1 medium tanks (Sherman II) moving forward to the Alamein line before the start of the offensive*

## Medium Tank M4A1

Standardised in December 1941, this was similar to the Medium M4, but had a cast hull which was curved to present less opportunity for a direct hit. This was the first of the M4 series to go into production. Very early models had Medium Tank M3 type bogie units, 75-mm M2 gun with counter weights and twin fixed machine-guns in the hull front; some of these vehicles arrived in England in 1942. The three-piece bolted front was later changed to a one-piece cast front. The British designation for this model was Sherman II. It was first used operationally in North Africa at El Alamein.

DATA

CREW  5

WEIGHT  33,180 kg  32.66 tons

HEIGHT  2.74 m  9 ft 0 in

LENGTH  5.89 m (M4)  19 ft 4 in
          5.84 m (M4A1)  19 ft 2 in

WIDTH  2.62 m  8 ft 7 in

ENGINE  Continental R975-C1 developing 353 hp

SPEED  Road 38.6 kmh  24 mph
      Cross-country 24-32 kmh  15-20 mph

ROAD RADIUS  193 km  120 miles

ARMAMENT  One 75-mm gun, two 0.30-cal
          (7.62-mm) Browning and one 0.50-cal
          (12.7-mm) Browning mgs

ROUNDS CARRIED  97 × 75 mm (M4)
                   90 × 75 mm (M4A1)
                   600 × 12.7 mm
                   4,750 × 7.62 mm

ARMOUR THICKNESS:  Max 75 mm  2.95 in
                     Min 12 mm  0.47 in

*Medium Tank M4A1 with one-piece cast front, in Northern New Guinea*

## Medium Tank M4A2

*M4A2 medium tanks in action with the Soviet forces*

The British designation for this version was Sherman III. It was generally similar to the Medium M4, except that it was powered by twin General Motors 6-71 Diesel engines; either engine could be operated independently. The second type to go into production, this version was supplied to the Soviets and to the British, first being used by the latter at the Battle of El Alamein. Late models of the M4A2 had 47 degree front armour plate, the differential housing was the cast one-piece round-nose type.

*Medium Tank M4A2 on Peleliu Island*

## Medium Tank M4A3

Standardised in January 1942, this vehicle was also similar to the M4, except that it was powered by a 500-hp Ford engine. This was an 8-cylinder liquid-cooled V-type engine that had been specifically designed for tanks. Early production models were equipped with the M34 gun mount and a cast one-piece round-nose differential housing. Late production models of the M4A3 were equipped with the 75-mm gun in the M34A1 gun mount and were fitted with a cast one-piece sharp-nosed differential housing. This was the fifth version of the M4 series to go into production and was the model most favoured by the US Army. Only a few M4A3s were supplied to other nations; those received by the British were known as Sherman IV.

*Early production model of Medium Tank M4A3 in service with the British Army. (Sherman IV)*

*Medium Tank M4A4 of US Army moving through German town of Weisweiler*

## Medium Tank M4A4

This was the fourth version to go into production, and was generally similar to the M4, but was powered by the Chrysler 5-line water-cooled tank engine. To install this engine it was necessary to lengthen the rear hull to give an overall length of 19 ft 10½ in (6.06 m). The 370-hp unit gave the vehicle a top speed of 25 mph (40 kmh). A longer track with 83 shoes was required, as compared to the 79 shoes fitted to the other models. Early M4A4 production types mounted the 75-mm gun in an M34 gun mount but this was replaced on late production vehicles with the M34A1 mount. The three-piece bolted differential housing was retained on all versions of the M4A4. This tank was the major type supplied to the British Army and was designated Sherman V.

*Sherman Vs of the Canadian Army in Holland. Note sections of tank tracks placed for extra protection*

# Medium Tank M4 (76 mm) Series

To improve the firepower of the M4 series to compete more effectively with the superior German tank guns, the M4 was equipped with the 76-mm M1A1 high velocity gun. The 76-mm gun was installed in a large cylindrical turret that had been developed for the T23 Medium Tank. Improvements in the gun development resulted in the M1A1C and M1A2 which were virtually identical to the original M1A1 except for the fitting of a muzzle brake. The 76-mm gun installation was standardised and introduced on production lines from February 1944, and vehicles so fitted were available in time for the Normandy landings and subsequent combat in NW Europe. The following M4 variants were fitted with the 76-mm' gun:

Medium Tank M4A1 (76 mm) Sherman II.

Medium Tank M4A2 (76 mm) Sherman III.

Medium Tank M4A3 (76 mm) Sherman IV.

Shermans armed with the 76-mm gun that were taken into service with the British Army were given the suffix A (Sherman IIA, Sherman IIIA and Sherman IVA).

*Medium Tanks M4A2 armed with 76-mm guns*

*Medium Tank M4A2 with 76-mm gun M1A2 and horizontal volute spring suspension*

# Medium Tanks M4 (105-mm howitzer) and M4A3 (105-mm howitzer)

DATA

CREW 5

WEIGHT 33,180 kg (M4) 32.66 tons
34,180 kg (M4A3) 33.64 tons

HEIGHT 2.82 m 9 ft 3 in

LENGTH 5.89 m (M4) 19 ft 4 in
5.90 m (M4A3) 19 ft 4¼ in

WIDTH 2.61 m 8 ft 7 in

ENGINE Continental R975-CI (M4)
Ford GAA (M4A3)

SPEED Road 38.6 kmh (M4) 24 mph
42 kmh (M4A3) 26 mph
Cross-country 24 to 32 kmh 15 to 20 mph

ROAD RADIUS 193 km 120 miles

ARMAMENT One 105-mm M4 howitzer, two
0.30-cal (7.62-mm) and one 0.50-cal
(12.7-mm) mgs

ROUNDS CARRIED 66×105 mm 300×12.7 mm
4,000×7.62 mm

ARMOUR THICKNESS Max 75 mm 2.95 in
Min 12 mm 0.47 in

This modification of Medium Tanks M4 and M4A3 was designed to combine the firepower of the 105-mm howitzer with the performance of a medium tank and were intended to replace the 75-mm Howitzer Motor Carriages, M8, in Medium Tank Battalion Headquarter Companies.

The 105-mm M4 howitzer was mounted in a Combination Gun Mount, M52, with a co-axial .30-cal Browning machine-gun. Other armaments were as in the M4 and M4A3. Both vehicles were fitted with the cast one-piece sharp-nose differential housing. Late production models of both versions had the vertical volute spring suspension changed to the wide track horizontal volute type. British designation for M4 (105-mm How) was Sherman IB and for the M4A3 (105-mm How) Sherman IVB. A few M4 (105-mm) vehicles with HVSS were taken into British service for trials; these were know as Sherman IBY.

*Early production model of M4 with 105-mm howitzer*

*Medium Tank M4A3E2 on the outskirts of Metz*

## Medium Tank M4A3E2

This was a compromise design proposed in early 1944 to fill the requirement for an assault vehicle for close support of infantry in the European Theatre of Operations. The basic vehicle was the Medium Tank M4A3 with more armour added to all hull surfaces giving a maximum thickness of 100 mm (3.94 in). A new heavy turret was designed with frontal armour of 150 mm (5.91 in). Because of the vehicles' increased weight, extended end connectors were used on the outsides of the tracks to improve the ride.

DATA

| | | | |
|---|---|---|---|
| CREW | 5 | ROAD RADIUS | 161 km   100 miles |
| WEIGHT | 41,910 kg   41.25 tons | ARMAMENT | One 75-mm gun, two 0.30-cal |
| HEIGHT | 3.43 m   11 ft 2⅞ in | | (7.62-mm) and one 0.50-cal (12.7-mm) |
| LENGTH | 6.27 m   20 ft 7 in | | mgs |
| WIDTH | 2.83 m   9 ft 3½ in | ROUNDS CARRIED | 106×75 mm   600×12.7 mm |
| ENGINE | Ford GAA developing 450 hp | | 6,250×7.62 mm |
| SPEED | Road 35.4 kmh   22 mph | ARMOUR THICKNESS | Max 100 mm   3.94 in |
| | Cross-country 24 to 32 kmh   15 to 20 mph | | Min   12 mm   0.47 in |

## Sherman 17-pdr Firefly

The major development of the M4 in British service was the fitting of the 17-pdr gun to a proportion of Shermans to provide the most powerfully armed British tank of the war. To achieve this the turret had to be slightly modified and the gun was mounted on its side and adapted for left-hand loading. The alterations to the turret were kept to a minimum and it was possible to use the existing trunnions together with a new gun mounting, recoil and elevating gear. The wireless set was transferred from inside the turret to an armoured box welded to the outside rear of the turret.

These up-gunned Shermans were ready in 1944 in time to take part in the invasion of Normandy. Several marks of the British Sherman tanks were used for the 17-pdr conversions and these received the suffix C; the most numerous of these was the Sherman VC known as Firefly.

*Sherman VC Medium Tank M4A4 with 17-pdr gun* ▼

*Sherman IC. Picture shows the late production model of the M4 with rolled and cast front hull and armed with the 17-pdr gun*

# Sherman DD Tanks

The DD (Duplex Drive) equipment was a flotation device invented by engineer Nicholas Straussler as a means of converting a standard tank into a temporary amphibious vehicle for river or sea crossing. The equipment was first tested in June 1941 on a Tetrarch light tank and production was started during 1942 on DD equipment for its adaptation to the Valentine tank. These vehicles, however, were only utilised in a training role, although a few Valentine DD tanks were used in Italy during 1945. By April 1943 the DD equipment had been developed for attachment to the Sherman tank.

This consisted of waterproofing the tank and fitting a collapsible canvas screen with rubber air tubes. This assembly was attached to a boat-shaped platform that was welded round the hull of the tank. The rubber tubes were filled with compressed air from two cylinders carried in the hull of the tank. On being inflated, the tubes raised the canvas screen which was locked into position by struts. When entering the water, the air-filled screen acted as a flotation device. Two small screw propellers, driven from the bevel drive of the vehicle, propelled the tank at approximately 4 knots. Steering was accomplished by swivelling the propellers to left or right. On reaching the shore, the air tubes were deflated causing the screen to collapse, and the vehicle reverted to its normal combat role. The twin screws were retractable for running on land.

Sherman DD tanks were used in the Normandy landings, for the Rhine crossing and in northern Italy in 1945.

Basic Sherman vehicles used for this conversion were the Sherman III (Medium M4A2) and Sherman V (Medium M4A4).

*Sherman DD tank crossing the Rhine*

*M4A1 Medium Tanks shown with Deep Water Fording device. It was used to increase the fording depth of tanks up to six feet in surf. British used a similar device*

# Heavy Tank M26 General Pershing

**DATA**

CREW 5

WEIGHT 45,900 kg 45.18 tons

HEIGHT 2.75 m 9 ft 1 in

LENGTH 8.79 m 28 ft 10 in

WIDTH 3.51 m 11 ft 6 in

ENGINE Ford GAF V-8 developing 500 hp

SPEED Road 32 kmh 20 mph

Cross-country 8.4 kmh 5.2 mph

ROAD RADIUS 148 km 92 miles

ARMAMENT One 90-mm M3 gun, two 0.30-cal (7.62-mm) and one 0.50-cal (12.7-mm) mgs

ROUNDS CARRIED 70×90 mm
500×12.7 mm
5,000×7.62 mm

ARMOUR THICKNESS Max 102 mm 4.02 in
Min 13 mm .51 in

The development of the Heavy Tank M26 resulted from the evolution of the T20 series of medium tanks that were intended to supplant the Medium M4. The constant insistences of the Ordnance Department upon increase of fire power in these vehicles resulted in the development of the Heavy Tanks T25E1 and T26E1. Heavy Tank T26E3 was the production model of T26E1, incorporating many improvements. Twenty of these vehicles were committed to combat in Europe before January 1945, and standardised as M26 in May 1945. The suspension was of the individually sprung torsion bar type, the armour was placed at varying angles to provide the greatest possible protection against projectiles. Armament consisted of a 90-mm M3 gun, mounted co-axially with a .30-cal machine-gun in the turret; the 90-mm gun was equipped with a muzzle brake. A .30-cal machine-gun was located in the bow, and a .50-cal machine-gun for anti-aircraft defence was mounted on the turret. Periscopes for all crew members and a two-way radio were provided. Used operationally in Europe and the Pacific (Okinawa).

*Heavy Tank M26 General Pershing, of the 11th Armored Division crossing Muhl river in Austria*

*Photo Credits*
P. Chamberlain
H. L. Doyle
Colonel R. J. Icks
Imperial War Museum
U.S. Official